MW00909965

FRANKLIN D. ROOSEVELT

FRANKLIN D. ROOSEVELT
MAN OF DESTINY

Rebecca Larsen

FRANKLIN WATTS
NEW YORK/LONDON/TORONTO/SYDNEY
1991

Photographs copyright ©: The Franklin D. Roosevelt Library: pp. 1, 2, 4, 7
top, 10, 11, 15 top; UPI/Bettmann Archive: pp. 3, 5, 6, 7 bottom, 8 top, 9, 12
top, 13, 14, 15 bottom, 16; AP/Wide World Photos: p. 8 bottom;
United Nations Photo: p. 12 bottom.

Library of Congress Cataloging-in-Publication Data

Larsen, Rebecca.
Franklin D. Roosevelt : Man of destiny / by Rebecca
Larsen.
p. cm.
Includes bibliographical references and index.
Summary: Discusses the life of the president who guided America
through such crises as the Great Depression and World War II.
ISBN 0-531-15231-6.—ISBN 0-531-11068-0 (lib. bdg.)
1. Roosevelt, Franklin D. (Franklin Delano), 1882–1945.
2. Presidents—United States—Biography. [1. Roosevelt, Franklin
D. (Franklin Delano), 1882–1945. 2. Presidents.] I. Title.
E807.1.L37 1991
973.917′092—dc20
[B]   91-17828 CIP AC

Contents

Preparing to play Franklin Roosevelt on stage, the actor Ralph Bellamy once asked Eleanor Roosevelt if her husband, Franklin, paralyzed by polio, crawled face down as he went about their home. "Never face down," she replied. "Always face up, in a sitting position, drawing his body after him. He deliberately did something to distract you, so that you were never conscious of seeing anything but that wonderful head."

1

"A splendid large baby boy"

It was a cold, dreary evening in the Hudson River valley, and the wind blew sharply through the pines and hemlocks of Springwood, the estate of James Roosevelt near Hyde Park, New York.

In an upstairs bedroom of the Roosevelt home, Roosevelt's young wife, Sara, had gone into labor. Throughout the night, she and her husband stayed awake waiting. At daybreak they summoned a doctor, but still the baby did not come. By evening, Sara's mother had arrived at the house but still the baby had not been born. Sara lay in agony in her heavy mahogany bed. Her screams frightened her husband and mother.

Finally, at eight that evening, the doctor administered chloroform to Sara, who sank into unconsciousness. Shortly after, her baby was delivered, blue and limp from the effects of the drug. The doctor breathed into the child's mouth to force open his lungs; finally, the baby turned pink and cried loudly.

Before going to bed that night, January 30, 1882, James Roosevelt wrote in his wife's diary, "At quarter to nine my Sallie had a splendid large baby boy. He weighs 10 lbs., without clothes.'' [1]

Sara named her child Franklin Delano after a favorite uncle. When the baby was christened, one of his godparents was Elliott Roosevelt, a distant cousin of James Roosevelt. In two years Elliott would become a father himself when his daughter, Eleanor—who would play a momentous role in Franklin's life—was born.

The Hudson River valley home that baby Franklin was born into was a comfortable one, well insulated by wealth and power and privilege from the great forces then changing the face of American society. It was a time when great numbers of immigrants were flooding into the United States from southern and eastern Europe and Asia—people whom many Americans considered undesirable. In the West, Americans had pushed their way to the Pacific Ocean, and there seemed to be no frontier left to conquer, no lands left to open up. More and more farmers were moving to town to work in the factories that were turning the United States into a major industrial power. By the end of the century the nation would surpass Great Britain in the production of iron and steel. The growth of factories had sparked formation of labor unions, which campaigned for shorter hours, better pay, and safer workplaces. Soon, hundreds of strikes would break out, most of them aimed at gaining an eight-hour day for workers.

There was political upheaval as well. Just a few months before Franklin's birth, President James A. Garfield, a Republican, had been assassinated. He was succeeded by Vice President Chester A. Arthur.

But life was placid and serene for the Roosevelts, who were descended from Dutch families who had come to New Amsterdam in the 1600s. Many of these early settlers of New York (the name was changed from New Amsterdam by the British) became wealthy merchants and intermarried with other wealthy families.

Franklin Roosevelt's father, James, was twenty-six years older than his wife, and in fact had a son, James,

11

from a previous marriage who was the same age as Sara. The elder James, who had been trained as a lawyer, lived like an English country squire on his estate, Springwood. But from time to time he ventured into the outside world, attempting to cash in on the trends in business of the times.

As industries grew, more and more smaller companies were merging into large companies that could dominate an entire industry. James Roosevelt and some of his friends tried to form a huge coal company to lock up most of the coal deposits in the Cumberland area of Kentucky. But a financial panic (depression) in 1873 and then a railroad strike caused huge losses for the company, and he and his friends were voted out of their leadership position by the stockholders.

The depression of the 1870s also ruined another of his ventures, an attempt to form a company to control all the railroads in the Southeast. He was also involved in trying to build a canal across Nicaragua to link the Atlantic and Pacific oceans. The venture would have been paid for by private investments. But the group also sought funding from the U.S. Congress. When the Nicaragua Canal bill failed to pass the House of Representatives, the plans fell apart. Later, of course, the U.S. government had a canal built across Panama.

Due to these financial failures, the Roosevelts never became as wealthy as some prominent families of the era— the Astors and the Vanderbilts and the Rockefellers. But still James Roosevelt's finances were secure. He still made money from coal and railroad holdings and commercial buildings. His new young wife, Sara, had even more money than he had. Her father, Warren Delano, had made a fortune in trade in China and also had mining interests.

Although Sara Roosevelt could have turned her baby over to his nursemaid, she doted on her only child. She nursed Franklin until he was a year old and kept a detailed diary of his every new word and doing, his happy moments and his sad ones. "Baby went to his first party yesterday . . . wanted to dance and I could hardly hold him" or "Baby walked quite alone. He is quite proud of his new accomplishment."[2]

She had a detailed schedule for each of his days and spent many hours playing games with him and reading stories. Sometimes her husband complained that she spent too much time hovering over Franklin.

Although he played sometimes with neighbor boys and with Taddy Roosevelt, the son of his older half brother, James, Franklin spent most of his time with adults. His mother did not allow him to talk to the lower- and middle-class children living in the village of Hyde Park.

James Roosevelt was devoted to his young son and took Franklin sledding, iceboating, and fishing at Springwood. Often, young Franklin followed his father about the 900-acre estate as James inspected his dairy cattle and trotting horses and looked over his crops. Franklin had his own Welsh pony, Debby, and several dogs, first a spitz named Budgy, then a Saint Bernard, a Newfoundland, and a red setter. He quickly learned to love the outdoors and the trees and fields of Springwood.

In spite of the attention lavished on him and the many toys and playthings he received, Franklin seems to have been obedient and hardworking and eager to please. Still, he disobeyed and rebelled at times. He sometimes pretended to be ill to avoid attending church on Sundays.

Once at dinner, he bit a piece out of a drinking glass and held it in his mouth until his mother took it out and threw it away. She scolded him, but when they returned to the table he did the same thing again. When Sara retrieved the second piece of glass, she asked him: "Franklin, where is your obedience?"

"My 'bedience," he replied, "has gone upstairs for a walk."[3]

His mother contended that she took special care not to spoil him. Once, at age four, he was racing toy horses with his mother. When his horse lost twice, he demanded that she turn over her horse to him. She agreed, but when he lost again, he became furious. Sara took all the toys away, telling him that she would not play with him again until he learned to behave. But she was not overly strict and rigid, and Franklin was rarely punished. "We took a secret pride in the fact that Franklin instinctively never seemed to require that kind of handling," she said.[4]

All the attention given to Franklin did not stem from great dreams that his parents had for him and his career. They fully expected that he would live a life like theirs— one of comfort and wealth—mingling with people of the same social set they belonged to. Most American mothers believe that their sons will grow up to be president, Sara Roosevelt said, but she did not. "What was my ambition for him? . . . to grow to be like his father, straight and honorable, just and kind, an outstanding American."[5]

Beginning when he was three, Franklin's parents took him regularly on their voyages across the Atlantic. In all, he made eight trips to Europe before age fifteen. There the Roosevelts mingled with royalty and high society. Franklin's father visited Bad Nauheim, a German spa that offered a water cure for his bad heart.

The Roosevelts also paid long visits to the estates of other family members in the Hudson River valley. Summers were spent in a seashore cottage on Campobello, a Canadian island off the coast of Maine, where many wealthy business people from the East Coast had built their summer homes. Sometimes the Roosevelts briefly rented homes in New York City or Washington, D.C., while James Roosevelt conducted business in those cities.

Although most of James Roosevelt's associates were members of the Republican party, he was a Democrat. The Democrats were not particularly different from the Republicans in their political views at that time, but still it went against the typical pattern for an aristocrat like James Roosevelt to support the Democratic party.

Once, when Franklin was five, his father took him to visit the Democratic president Grover Cleveland. Cleveland seemed sad and worn to young Franklin. At the time he was battling Congress over pension bills. Cleveland patted

Franklin's head and said quite seriously, "My little man, I am making a strange wish for you. It is that you may never be President of the United States."[6]

With all the traveling that the Roosevelts did, Franklin's early schooling took place in bits and pieces. The Roosevelts hired governesses for their son, some of whom came and went very quickly.

Despite his haphazard education, Franklin was a quick and eager student who quickly surpassed other youngsters his age. He became fluent in French and German in grade school. He read widely and loved books about naval battles and sea travel.

When Franklin was nine, his father bought a 51-foot sailing yacht, the *Half Moon,* which was kept at Campobello. Soon Franklin was sailing the boat himself with his mother as a passenger. At sixteen he received a 21-foot sailing boat, the *Full Moon,* for his very own.

Like many children he liked to collect things, only he did it on almost an adult level. He had a huge stamp collection, part of which he received from his mother, who had spent many years collecting stamps in her travels around the world. Franklin spent hours studying the stamps under a magnifying glass and pasting them into albums filled with notes.

He loved birds and gathered eggs and nests and kept careful diaries of his sightings. Then he decided to shoot and stuff a sample of every species of bird in Dutchess County, the county where he lived. At the time such interests were thought admirable, regardless of what it meant to the birds. So when Franklin was eleven, his father gave him a gun that Franklin used to kill members of more than 300 species of birds. At first he gutted and stuffed his specimens, even though he found the task repulsive. Once he was sure he could do the taxidermy himself if he had to, he shipped the birds off to a professional taxidermist. His collection of Hudson River valley birds was the most extensive ever assembled.

Franklin was the central focus of the lives of his mother

15

and father, and it was difficult for them to finally send him to boarding school, where so many youngsters in their social group went. The usual age for such boys to go to preparatory school was twelve, but the Roosevelts kept Franklin at home with governesses and tutors until he was fourteen.

In the fall of 1896, after the Roosevelts took one of their usual trips to Europe, they set out by train and horse and buggy for Groton, a new and prestigious school in Massachusetts. Traveling with them was Taddy Roosevelt, who was also enrolling at Groton. After leaving Franklin behind, Sara Roosevelt wrote in her diary, "It is hard to leave our darling boy." [7]

For Franklin, a rather shy boy who had spent most of his life with adults, being thrust into the world of Groton required some adjustments. Most of the other eighteen boys in Franklin's class had already been at the school for two years and had made fast friendships.

Although Groton was a school for the wealthy, it was not a luxurious place. Each boy slept in a tiny, simple cubicle on a hard-mattressed bed. The showers before breakfast were icy cold, and the boys complained frequently about the food. They rose at seven and went to class until mid-afternoon each day. Franklin took Latin, Greek, algebra, literature, French, composition, history and science. There were also studies of Bible history and missions.

The central figure in his tight little academic world was the school's rector, Endicott Peabody, an Episcopal clergyman of strong personality, steadfast faith in God, and great character and energy. He had almost singlehandedly founded the school. He aimed to give a thorough intellectual education, grounded in Christian principles, to upper-class boys, who would then be ready for college and service in the outside world.

Boys at the school admired and respected Peabody and also feared him a little. As an adult, Franklin Roosevelt would later say, "As long as I live, the influence of

Dr. and Mrs. Peabody means and will mean more to me than that of any other people next to my father and mother."[8]

Often, in his chapel talks, Peabody urged the young men in the school to enter politics and government service, even though very few were likely to do so. For the most part, their families expected them to enter the world of business and finance.

When boys misbehaved at the school, teachers or older students gave out "black marks." An individual black mark meant that a boy had to rake leaves or shovel snow; a block of six marks at once meant he had to visit Rector Peabody for a lecture—a punishment the boys greatly feared.

Although most boys got two or three marks every week, Franklin received none at all until near the end of his first year. He got his first mark for talking in class. "I am very glad I got it," he wrote his parents, "as I was thought to have no school spirit before."[9]

Older Groton boys often inflicted stiffer punishments on younger boys for cheating or other offenses that had not been reported to teachers. Sometimes older boys forced younger ones to serve time sitting scrunched up in the boxes in which they kept their shoes. At other times the offending boy was dragged to the bathroom, where basins of water were poured down his throat for eight to ten seconds. Franklin managed to avoid all this.

Frail and slight, he longed to succeed in the sports that counted at Groton, like football, baseball, and crew. But he did poorly at them. In the spring he was put on a team of the school's worst baseball players, called the BBBB, or Bum Base Ball Boys.

His greatest athletic accomplishment was in the high kick. In this unusual sport a tin pan was hung by a cord from the ceiling and a boy would leap in the air and kick at it. After each round of kicks the pan was raised a little higher in the air. As the pan rose higher and higher, after each kick the kicker fell on the floor. Franklin once won the event with a kick of 7 feet 3½ inches. He wrote his parents: "At every kick I landed on my *neck* on the left side so the result is that the whole left side of my body is sore and my left arm is a little swollen."[10]

His first-year grades were above average but not outstanding; he failed one final exam in Greek and got only a 65 in geometry. But throughout his four years at Groton he usually ranked in the upper fourth or fifth of his class.

As Franklin went through Groton, he grew more interested in the outside world—particularly the Caribbean, where there was a chance that the United States might wage war on Spain over Cuba. Spain owned Cuba, but Americans had many business interests on the island. Americans grew angry about reports that the Spanish were mistreating the Cubans, who wanted independence. Then an explosion destroyed the U.S. battleship *Maine* in Havana harbor, and 260 American sailors died. American newspapers blamed the Spanish, although it was unclear what had actually happened. Congress declared war on Spain on April 11, 1898.

When war was declared, Franklin noted in a journal he was keeping: "War began today! . . . and of course, everyone is wildly excited."[11]

He and two friends even planned to run off to Boston to join the Navy. But on the day of the proposed escape, all three came down with scarlet fever and ended up in the school infirmary.

Unable to join the excitement, Franklin followed the exploits of his older distant cousin Theodore Roosevelt. When the war began, Theodore, or Teddy, as he was often called, resigned as assistant secretary of the navy to join a cavalry regiment called the Rough Riders. With Theodore Roosevelt as their leader, the Rough Riders made a famous charge up San Juan Hill in Cuba against the Spanish. The charge lacked military form and irritated regular Army officers who led an orderly advance that captured the San Juan blockhouse. But Roosevelt's bravado and courage impressed reporters, who helped turn Teddy into a national hero.

The war ended quickly with the Spanish giving in to most of the demands of the United States. Theodore Roosevelt was soon running for governor of New York. Although James Roosevelt was a Democrat and Teddy was a Republican, James supported Teddy. Franklin got caught up in the campaign. "We were all wild with delight when we heard of Teddy's election," he wrote to his parents. "The whole dormitory went mad." [12]

In his final year at Groton some boys found Franklin cocky and sarcastic; others thought he was merely confident and self-assured. That year he was named a dormitory prefect in charge of thirty-six younger boys. He became manager of the baseball team, a job that required long, hard hours of setting up the diamond and handling the team's equipment.

Like many young men at Groton, he planned to go on to Harvard. Because he had already passed some preliminary exams for college, he was allowed to take college classes in his last year at Groton. That way he could finish his degree at Harvard in three years instead of four.

In June 1899, at Groton's graduation, he won the Latin Prize. His reward was a forty-volume set of Shakespeare. Rector Peabody's final written statement to Franklin's parents was: "He has been a thoroughly faithful scholar & a most satisfactory member of this school throughout his course. I part with Franklin with reluctance." [13]

2

"I am very busy"

Franklin's chosen college, Harvard University, the then all-male school in Cambridge, Massachusetts, was the alma mater of presidents and poets and philosophers—John Quincy Adams, Ralph Waldo Emerson, and William James, to name a few. Brilliant professors headed the faculty, and many taught Roosevelt.

Yet although Harvard students were a special group, there were elites within the elite. From the beginning, his family background and wealth and his schooling at Groton put Franklin Roosevelt into the most privileged class at Harvard.

As a freshman, Roosevelt was tall and slender—he carried only 146 pounds on a 6-foot 1½-inch-tall frame. He had his mother's handsome chiseled profile and a quick smile. Women were attracted to him, but although he went to parties with them, he had no serious romances. He was still very close to his parents, particularly his mother, who tried to anticipate his every wish.

At Harvard, Roosevelt and a friend from Groton, Lathrop Brown, rented a three-room suite in a privately owned dormitory in an area called the Gold Coast. His mother helped him furnish the suite, where he hung pennants and photographs from Groton. Most of his meals he ate with former Groton students.

He loaded up on courses, deciding to major in history and political science and minor in English composition and literature. But Roosevelt's main interests were not his classes. At the end of a half year, he had a C+ in geology, B− in French prose and poetry, B in history, and D+ in Latin.

He did just enough studying to get by while making friends and joining clubs and teams. When he arrived at Groton, he had been a shy, quiet boy, trying to please the adults in charge and fit in with his classmates. At Harvard he was sharp, witty, and aggressive, determined to succeed.

Despite his slight build, he tried out for sports, ending up on a scrub team in football and an intramural boating team. But he was elected captain of both teams. He made the freshman glee club and became its secretary. Out of enthusiasm for his cousin Theodore Roosevelt, running for vice president, Franklin Roosevelt joined the Harvard Republican Club and marched in a torchlight parade supporting the William McKinley–Theodore Roosevelt ticket.

His biggest success was on the Harvard *Crimson,* the school's student newspaper. He was one of dozens of young men who tried out for the paper; his goal was to win a post as one of the editors by the end of his college career. "I am trying for the 'Crimson,' " he wrote to his parents, "& if I work hard for two years I may be made an editor. I have to make out notices & go to interviews so I am very busy." [1]

He became so busy that by the spring of freshman year he was working six hours a day at the *Crimson.*

While working as a reporter, he got one big scoop. He found out that Teddy Roosevelt, by then the new vice president, would be speaking on campus to a government

21

class. The government professor wanted to keep all this a secret, but Franklin rushed a story into print. As a result, 2,000 people showed up at the lecture hall to hear Teddy. The professor was angry, but the *Crimson* staff was delighted and Franklin was elected as one of the paper's five editors for the next year.

Amid the turmoil and excitement of his freshman year, Franklin Roosevelt faced personal sorrow. On December 8, 1900, after several months in which he grew progressively weaker due to heart disease, James Roosevelt died at age seventy-two.

After his father's death, Franklin's mother, Sara, only forty-six, seemed to cling even more tightly to her son. Eventually, she rented an apartment in Boston so that she could be near her son during the school term. Franklin still remained attached to Sara, but he grew anxious to break free, to become more independent.

The summer after his freshman year, Franklin accompanied his mother on a tour of Europe. It was a trip he hoped would ease her grief over his father's death. They sailed in July and went to Germany, Norway, Switzerland, and France. Just before their return home in early September, they learned that President McKinley had been shot by an assassin during the Pan-American Exposition in Buffalo. By the time the Roosevelts reached New York, McKinley had died, making Franklin's cousin Theodore the new president of the United States.

Although the Roosevelts and the entire country were shocked and grieved, it thrilled Franklin that his cousin had reached the White House. Not only did the spotlight fall on Theodore Roosevelt, it also fell on his family, including Franklin. Franklin's social life and school activities fascinated the Boston newspapers, who often compared his career at Harvard to Teddy's.

But Franklin soon fell short of Theodore in one important social achievement. In the fall of his sophomore year, the elite clubs at Harvard began choosing members.

Franklin was chosen for Delta Kappa Epsilon, also known as D.K.E. or Dickey. Another set of clubs then picked members from those in Dickey. Most prestigious of all of these was the Porcellian, nicknamed the Pig Club.

To get into this club system, a student usually had to come from a prestigious and wealthy family and had to be a graduate of the "right" preparatory school. As a Roosevelt who had gone to Groton, Franklin had every right to expect that he could make the list for the Porcellian. Not only that: cousin Theodore, now president, had belonged to the Pig Club.

But it was not to be—the Pig Club rejected him.

Franklin's social standing on campus might have been tainted by a scandal involving Taddy, his nephew and the son of Franklin's half brother, James. Just after Franklin had arrived at Harvard, Taddy, a poor student anyway, had eloped to Florida with a New York City dance hall girl. The marriage ended in divorce, and Taddy returned to New York to work for the Salvation Army to make up for his disgrace.

Newspapers around the country turned the scandal into front-page news. It was not the kind of incident designed to enhance Franklin's standing among the Harvard aristocrats.

Not making a college club seems a minor tragedy. But some, including Eleanor Roosevelt, who became Franklin's wife, contended that this rejection by the Pig Club meant a great deal to Franklin and for the first time showed him what it was like to be an underdog and a victim of injustice.

Others said it was not a great blow. According to a friend of his from Harvard, "his not making the Porcellian meant only that he was free of any possible restraining influence of a lot of delightful people who thought that the world belonged to them and who did not want to change anything in it." [2]

At any rate, Franklin soon joined a slightly less exclusive club, Alpha Delta Phi, also known as the Fly Club. Whatever hurt feelings he had, he set them aside and became very active in his new club.

By the spring of 1903, because of the courses he had taken in advance at Groton, Roosevelt had earned his bachelor's degree and received his diploma. He had finished his undergraduate work in only three years, but with a C-plus average, considered very respectable among young men of his social class. But he wasn't about to leave Harvard behind yet because he had been elected to the prestigious post of president, or editor in chief, of the Harvard *Crimson*. He was not about to give up this reward for all his years of labor on the paper.

To stay on campus he decided to enter the Harvard graduate school and enrolled in history and economics courses. He did not intend, however, to actually earn a master's degree, but, he wrote his mother, "the courses will do me lots of good, whether I get B or D in them."[3]

As president of the *Crimson,* he wrote all the newspaper's editorials. Franklin's family ties meant that he personally knew many important political figures. These associations plus his education had made him familiar with many key political and economic questions of the day. Yet most of his editorials in the final year on the *Crimson* focused on the problems of the Harvard football team, a lightweight topic for someone who would one day become one of the most important men in the world.

After the Harvard team squeaked by Carlisle College by a score of 12–11, Franklin caused a major ruckus on campus with an editorial saying that student spectators were "weary of the slow, listless play of certain men in the line, who seem to think that their weight is a sufficient certificate of admission to membership on a university team."[4]

He did campaign for some campus reforms. One of his editorials recommended that a more democratic system be adopted for picking class officers. Generally, the campus clubs put up slates of their own men, who were easily elected. It was some time before the system changed. Roosevelt himself was elected to an important post, permanent chairman of the class committee.

More than school activities were on Franklin's mind in those last months at Harvard. He had fallen in love with the tall and willowy Anna Eleanor Roosevelt, his fifth cousin once removed and the daughter of his godfather, Elliott Roosevelt. Anna Eleanor, called Eleanor by her family, was also the niece of the president, Theodore Roosevelt.

Since childhood, Franklin had often seen Eleanor at family gatherings. Once, at a Christmas party when she was an awkward and gangly fourteen, she had stood nervously at the edge of the dance floor. She felt completely out of place in her long braids and a dress that was too short for her. Franklin, then sixteen years old, had asked her to dance, and she remembered his kindness for the rest of her life. As time went on, they continued to meet socially and their friendship grew.

While Franklin had been the child of parents who doted on his every wish and interest, Eleanor had been a neglected orphan. Her parents separated when she was quite young, primarily because her father, Elliott, brother of the president, had a severe drinking problem. Shortly after that, Eleanor's mother, Anna, died of diphtheria. Eleanor's grandmother took in Eleanor and her two younger brothers, and the children saw their father only occasionally. Despite his alcoholism and irresponsibility, Eleanor idolized her father. She longed for him to finally make a home for her as he promised to do. When she was ten, her dreams were shattered. He was badly injured in a fall and died a lonely and broken man whose family had lost faith in him.

The quiet and serious Eleanor lived a lonely, loveless life in her grandmother's house in New York City. Constant upheaval rocked the household, in part because two of Eleanor's uncles drank heavily and sometimes became violent. Although money had been left in trust for Eleanor and her brothers, her grandmother scrimped in caring for them.

Eleanor was rarely allowed to visit with friends outside the home. She also hesitated to invite friends to visit her grandmother's house. "My mother would ask me to go to have supper with Eleanor," said one of her cousins. "I never wanted to go. The grim atmosphere of that house. There was no place to play games, unbroken gloom everywhere. We ate our suppers in silence. The general attitude was 'don't do this.' "[5]

The gloom lifted when Eleanor went away to school in England at age fifteen. At a school called Allenwood, in the suburbs of London, she studied under a remarkable Frenchwoman, Mademoiselle Marie Souvestre, who encouraged Eleanor's confidence in herself and her interest in public affairs and politics.

Returning home at age eighteen, Eleanor was expected to be the typical rich-girl debutante. But she was interested in reaching out to the world, particularly to the poor and underprivileged. As a young woman in high society, she joined the Junior League, a group that besides its social activities did work in New York's settlement houses. These were small community centers in poor neighborhoods that provided classes and recreation for immigrant groups.

Eleanor taught calisthenics and dancing to immigrant Italian children. She also toured tenements and sweatshops to investigate conditions.

These activities were intermixed with parties, of course, and visits to the estates of friends. During 1903 her relationship with Franklin Roosevelt grew deeper and more serious. They exchanged visits and letters; on weekends Franklin checked on the well-being of Eleanor's brother Hall, who had enrolled at Groton.

On one visit to Groton, on November 22, 1903, Franklin proposed marriage to Eleanor. At first Eleanor was stunned and worried, filled with questions about what marriage would mean to her and her family. She could not believe that Franklin was serious. He seemed sure of himself, but did he actually mean marriage "for life, for death"?[6] But she was also eager to experience life to its fullest. "There seemed to me to be a necessity for hurry; without rhyme or reason I felt the urge to be a part of the stream of life and so [Franklin's proposal] seemed an entirely natural thing, and I never even thought that we were rather young and inexperienced."[7]

Many writers have debated about what drew Franklin to Eleanor and why he was anxious to marry at such a young age.

Certainly she was tall and graceful and known for her lovely blue eyes and blond hair. But her prominent teeth, which her grandmother could have had fixed if she had cared to spend the money, meant that Eleanor would never be considered a beauty.

Some have speculated that Franklin's intense admiration for Eleanor's uncle, Theodore Roosevelt, might also have played a role. The president considered Eleanor his favorite niece, and Franklin may have been drawn to her through a desire to draw closer to the circle of power surrounding Theodore.

Although Franklin seemed confident and self-assured to his male classmates at Harvard, many found him shy and insecure around women. Certainly he had known many other young women in his social class, but he had had only one serious relationship with a woman, an attractive Boston debutante, who broke up with him shortly before he grew more involved with Eleanor.

For both of them, Eleanor and Franklin, marriage also represented an escape from confining family ties. For Franklin, it meant a chance to take control of his life away from his mother; for Eleanor, it meant a chance to leave behind the dreary, sometimes frightening life in the home of her grandmother.

3

"A very real chance to be president"

Over Thanksgiving in 1903, Franklin and his mother, Sara, went to Fairhaven, the estate of Sara's brother in the Hudson River valley. There, Franklin told his mother privately that he loved Eleanor and planned to marry her.

Sara Roosevelt was shocked and hurt. "Franklin gave me quite a startling announcement," she wrote in her journal.[1]

He was too young to get married, she told him. She had also hoped that after leaving college he would spend more time with her to fill the gap left by the death of her husband.

Although she had invited Eleanor to her home many times and had often seen her at parties, she had no idea of her son's close relationship with Eleanor—perhaps because Franklin had wanted her not to know. And there were many questions in her mind about Eleanor as well. After all Eleanor was the daughter of an alcoholic and had been raised in a family setting filled with turmoil. Eleanor was even younger than Franklin.

Both Franklin and Eleanor assured Sara that she had

nothing to fear from their marriage. "I know just how you feel & how hard it must be," Eleanor told her in a letter, "but I do so want you to learn to love me a little." [2]

She would not only have a son now, Franklin told his mother, but also a daughter. "Dearest Mama," he wrote her, "I know what pain I must have caused you and you know I wouldn't do it if I really could have helped it. . . . I know my mind, have known for a long time. . . . Result: I am the happiest man just now in the world. . . ." [3]

But Sara insisted that he and Eleanor keep their romance a secret for a while.

In February 1904, Sara took Franklin and his college roommate Lathrop Brown on a six-week tour of the Caribbean—in spite of Franklin's graduate classes at Harvard. Franklin enjoyed the trip, but he did not forget Eleanor.

Gradually, Sara Roosevelt grew resigned to the marriage. In June, Franklin attended commencement for the class of 1904, which he considered his class although he had actually received a diploma the year before. Sara invited Eleanor to be there. Together they watched proudly while Franklin in cap and gown sat on the platform with other class officers.

That summer the young couple visited at Campobello and Hyde Park. In the fall Franklin and his mother moved to New York City, where he could attend Columbia Law School, a school then trying to build its faculty and reputation. He had considered going to Harvard's law school, but in New York he could be closer to Eleanor. His social calendar was loaded with parties and events, and his classwork suffered. The first year alone he was absent seventy-three times. He made few friends in the law school; for the most part he still socialized with the men he had met at Groton and Harvard.

Finally, at Thanksgiving, Franklin and Eleanor announced their engagement, and the wedding was set for the following spring. On the afternoon of March 17, 1905, some 200 guests gathered at the home of one of Eleanor's aunts in New York City. Outside on the street, hundreds of spectators and reporters gathered—not to see the bride and groom but to catch a glimpse of Theodore Roosevelt, president of the United States, who was to give the bride away.

In a satin gown covered with Brussels lace, Eleanor glided down a staircase on the arm of her uncle Teddy and met Franklin under a bower of palms and pink roses. There Endicott Peabody, Franklin's headmaster at Groton, conducted the ceremony for the young lovers.

After rings were exchanged, the young couple chatted with guests in the drawing room, but they were quickly left standing alone. Most of the crowd had flocked off with jolly Uncle Teddy to the dining room for refreshments.

That evening Franklin and Eleanor went to Hyde Park for a week's stay at Springwood. Then they returned to a New York City apartment. But once Franklin finished his classes at Columbia, they left on a more exciting honeymoon, a summer in Europe.

In France, England, Italy, and Germany, they were entertained by aristocrats and intellectuals. Along the way they wrote two or three letters a week to Franklin's mother. While they were gone, Franklin's mother rented and redecorated a house for them in New York City. Sara Roosevelt had agreed to their marriage, but she was determined to play an important role in Franklin's life and for many years dominated Eleanor and her household.

In Paris, Franklin received bad news from law school. He had gotten two B's but failed two classes. He wrote to his mother: "It certainly shows the uncertainty of marks, for I had expected much lower marks in some of the others and failure in one and thought I had done as well on the two I failed as in those I passed with B."[4]

His mother sent him his books so that he could study for makeup exams being held in the fall. When the couple returned to New York, Eleanor spurred Franklin to study harder. He passed the tests and stayed in law school until the spring of 1907. Then he passed the bar examination that entitled him to begin practicing law. At that point he dropped out of law school without finishing his degree to become a law clerk with the New York firm of Carter, Ledyard and Milburn.

Although this Wall Street firm was prestigious and had many large corporate clients, he started at the bottom. The first year he worked for no pay. After that he received a token salary for the tedious and routine job. He looked up cases in the law library, took papers to court and to county offices, and kept a list of cases for the partners in the firm.

Eventually he was allowed to try minor cases in the municipal courts. Often he defended large companies against claims filed by small businessmen or individuals. For the first time in his life, he mixed regularly with the lower classes, people in trouble with the law or with money problems.

He could very easily have made a comfortable career as a Wall Street lawyer. But already he had other goals.

One day, while sitting with his fellow law clerks at their rolltop desks, he told the group that he did not want to practice law forever. "I remember him saying . . . that he intended to run for office at the first opportunity and that he wanted to be and thought he had a very real chance to be president," one clerk recalled later.[5]

He had his career all mapped out: first a seat in the New York State Assembly, then service as assistant secretary of the navy, just like Theodore Roosevelt, then election as governor of New York.

During his three years at the law firm, Franklin and Eleanor built a family life for themselves, but it was an unusual household closely tied to Franklin's mother. On May 3, 1906, Franklin and Eleanor's first child, Anna Eleanor Roosevelt, was born. Over the first ten years of their marriage, they had six children in all.

Franklin had some money left to him by his father.

31

Eleanor had income of from $5,000 to $8,000 a year from a trust fund. The total was enough to provide a comfortable life including servants. But it was not enough to pay for a summer house at Campobello, a yacht, expensive clubs for Franklin, and costly trips—all part of their lifestyle.

So Sara Roosevelt, who controlled most of the fortune left by James Roosevelt, paid many of their expenses. One of her magnificent gifts was a pair of town houses she had built at East Sixty-fifth Street in New York. Sara arranged all the details with the architect and chose the furniture for the houses. She lived in one home, and Franklin and Eleanor lived in the other. Although Franklin and Eleanor paid her no rent, title to their house remained in her name. The two homes were joined by doors between their drawing rooms. Often Sara burst through the doors into the house of the young couple with no warning. She helped pick out their servants and made many decisions about raising the Roosevelt children.

A few weeks after the Roosevelts moved, Eleanor burst into tears as she sat at the dressing table of her beautiful new home. When Franklin asked what was wrong, Eleanor told him she "did not like to live in a house which was not in any way mine, one that I had done nothing about." [6]

Franklin was baffled and upset. Although he did not enjoy his mother telling him what to do, he could often get what he wanted from her. He did not resent his mother's interference in the same way that Eleanor did.

But although Franklin allowed his mother to dominate his wife, he cared deeply about Eleanor and his children. In 1908 on a business trip, he wrote home to Eleanor: "Loads of love as always and kiss the chicks. My one regret is that you aren't with me . . ." [7] His pet name for his children was "the chicks"; he called Eleanor by the nickname "Babs."

In 1910 Franklin's chance to enter politics finally came when Democratic party officials from the Hudson River valley approached him about running for state senator. Although Franklin had voted Republican in past presidential elections in order to support his cousin Theodore, he remained at heart a Democrat, like his father. Although he lived in New York City for his job, he still visited often at the Roosevelt estate at Hyde Park and voted there as well.

The district that Roosevelt ran in comprised Dutchess, Putnam, and Columbia counties, a heavily Republican area. For over thirty-two years, various Republicans had been state senator there. His chance of winning seemed slim. But Franklin did have the power of the Roosevelt name behind him and the money to pay for a campaign. Both made him an attractive candidate to the Democratic officials.

Things were rocky for Eleanor and Franklin at the time. In the fall of 1909 their third child, Franklin Jr., only eighteen months old, had died of pneumonia. From birth, Franklin Jr. had been a sickly baby with heart problems. After his death, Eleanor grieved long and deeply even though she bore another son, Elliott, in the fall of 1910. Franklin more easily accepted the baby's death as a misfortune he could not control.

This situation must have weighed on Roosevelt's mind as he prepared for the 1910 campaign. But he loved new challenges and adventures. He plunged eagerly into the campaign. In a speech to Democrats at the nominating convention, he said: "We have real issues and an excellent platform to lay before the people, and with the aid of the independent thinking voters of these counties we have little to fear from the result on November eighth." [8]

Soon Roosevelt hit the roads of his district in a rented red Maxwell touring car. His fellow Democrats had discouraged his use of a car for fear that lower-class voters would think he was showing off his money. But Roosevelt wanted to cover as much territory as possible in the brief month before the election.

In his early speeches Roosevelt was hesitant and shy,

but he got tips on public speaking from Richard E. Connell, the Democratic candidate for Congress, who accompanied him. Connell had run before for Congress and lost every time, but he was famous for his fiery patriotic speeches. The two traveled from village to village, country store to country store, making about ten speeches a day and chatting with the local farmers, many of them Republicans, whose votes they desperately needed. The aristocratic young Roosevelt mingled eagerly each day with the masses and sought favors from those whom his mother considered beneath them.

Just his appearance must have alienated some voters. He often threw his head back and looked down through his pince-nez (eyeglasses that clip onto the nose) in a way that made him seem proud and arrogant. But he was also energetic and lively and concerned about farm problems. His interest and warmth won friends.

One other factor favored him. The country was growing dissatisfied with the Republicans who ran Congress and with William Howard Taft who had succeeded the popular Theodore Roosevelt as president. Voters seemed ready to make a change.

In his speeches Franklin Roosevelt stressed that he was an independent candidate, not tied to party bosses or special interests even in the Democratic party. He particularly liked a quote from Abraham Lincoln: "I am not bound to win, but I am bound to be true. I am not bound to succeed, but I am bound to live up to what light I have. I must stand with anybody that stands right and part with him when he goes wrong."[9]

On November 8, 1910, Roosevelt was elected to the state Senate by a vote of 15,708 to 14,568 for his opponent, Republican John F. Schlosser. It was a Democratic sweep in New York State. Richard Connell, the perennial congressional candidate, finally won office. The new governor was also Democratic, and Democrats took over both houses of the legislature.

With his usual wholehearted delight in a new challenge, Roosevelt moved his wife and children to a rented home in the state capital of Albany. Very few legislators could afford this on their annual salaries of only $1,500. Most lived in Albany hotels when the legislature was in session, and had to go home to work when it was not. But Roosevelt, with his independent family income, had no such problems and wanted to devote himself completely to his new job.

The day of the new governor's inauguration the Roosevelts held a big party for residents of their district, and hundreds poured into their new home to eat chicken salad sandwiches.

As a new senator, Roosevelt had strong views about what his mission should be. Part of it was to oppose the party bosses—the Tammany Hall Democrats from New York City. During the nineteenth century, the Tammany Society had grown into a powerful political machine that dealt out jobs and services to the poor and lower classes in New York City and in turn controlled the votes of those it helped. Tammany leaders decided who would run for office, and some were not above taking bribes in return for their influence on voters, city politicians, and the legislature.

The storm clouds built as the 1911 legislature debated who would be the new U.S. senator from New York State. At that time, before the Seventeenth Amendment was added to the Constitution, the state legislatures, not the voters, chose the senators. To win election in New York, a candidate had to receive a total of 101 votes, a majority of the legislators in both houses in New York.

Tammany and its boss, Charles F. Murphy, favored William "Blue-Eyed Billy" Sheehan for the job. Other Democrats thought Sheehan was an unsavory candidate and preferred election of a more progressive man, Edward M. Shepard, a lawyer and advocate of clean government in New York City.

Roosevelt, eager to show his independence of Tammany Hall, led the fight against Sheehan. Night after night a small band of legislators met at Roosevelt's Albany home to plot a rebellion against Tammany. When the first vote on the senator was taken in the legislature, Sheehan received 91 votes, not enough to win but close.

Soon the news about the fight against Tammany Hall spread to the front pages of newspapers across the country, and stories focused on Roosevelt. The *New York World* wrote: "A distant relative of Col. Roosevelt, he is thirty-two years of age, of spare figure and lean intellectual face, suggesting in appearance a student of divinity rather than a practical politician. Gold bowed spectacles loop his long, thin nose and a frock coat drapes his figure." [10]

Vote after vote was taken, and the legislature remained deadlocked. The Tammany politicians spread rumors that Roosevelt was anti-Catholic and anti-Irish. They put financial pressure on the insurgents. Some banks threatened to foreclose on the mortgages of homes of the rebel legislators, but still they held out.

But after ten weeks it began to look as if those Republican legislators whose support both Democratic groups needed to win the election might go along with the Tammany Hall Democrats. The rebels and their leader, Roosevelt, decided to compromise and accept another Tammany candidate, state Supreme Court justice James A. O'Gorman. Although O'Gorman was an organization man, he also had a respectable record as a judge. O'Gorman was elected, to wild cheers from the Tammany legislators, who believed they had crushed Roosevelt and the rebels.

Somewhat battered, Roosevelt still felt that the battle had been worth it. "There can be no question but that he sincerely felt he was doing a great service in making a spectacular battle against the party organization," said Frances Perkins, who had been lobbying in the legislature for better working conditions for women while Roosevelt was leading his crusade. "He won the battle, but it did not leave him with many friends in the Senate or Democratic

36

party."[11] Roosevelt later told Perkins: "You know, I was an awfully mean cuss when I first went into politics."[12]

Although Roosevelt and the insurgents did not win, their fight dramatized the need to have voters, rather then legislatures, pick senators. Roosevelt also received nationwide publicity for his respectability and honesty, and in his district the voters thought that he had fought a good and important fight.

As for his enemies in Tammany Hall, although he still opposed them on many issues, he also learned that many of these politicians were more in touch with the common man than he was. Eventually, he would decide he had to make peace with Tammany Hall if he wanted to further his political career.

In general, in the legislature Roosevelt focused mainly on the issues that worried his constituents—such matters as conservation of timber and the prices paid to farmers for crops. Already Roosevelt had decided that government had to step in and right wrongs in society even though it might infringe at times on the liberty of citizens to do as they pleased.

He had little if any concern about the common laborer and social reforms, according to Frances Perkins, who sought his support for a bill to cut the work week for women to fifty-four hours. Roosevelt did not actually support the bill, Perkins said, although the supposedly corrupt politicians of Tammany Hall did. "I took it hard that a young man who had so much spirit did not do so well in this," Perkins said.[13]

Later in life, he claimed that he had campaigned strongly for the bill. It was typical of him to change and revise his account of events in his past that he was not happy with. But records seem to indicate that he was absent when the actual vote was taken.

Soon after he went to Albany, Roosevelt met Woodrow Wilson, who became governor of New Jersey in 1910. He deeply admired Wilson, a former president of Princeton University, and his humanitarian ideals. And like Theodore Roosevelt, Wilson became a hero for Roosevelt. Wilson favored social and economic reforms that alienated Democratic party bosses. He called his program of reforms the "New Freedom." In spite of opposition from old-time politicians, Wilson became a candidate for the Democratic nomination for president in 1912, and Roosevelt was one of his most ardent supporters.

In June of that year, Roosevelt went to the Democratic convention in Baltimore to work for Wilson. A bitter struggle began between followers of Wilson and Champ Clark, the Speaker of the U.S. House of Representatives. Ballot after ballot was taken and no decision was reached. In his energetic way Roosevelt lobbied delegates for Wilson votes and organized rallies. Some say he put on a crucial rally for Wilson at a time when it seemed likely that Clark would win. Others say his efforts had little effect on the final vote, although they impressed Wilson.

Finally, the powerful Democrat William Jennings Bryan endorsed Wilson, and the governor of New Jersey won the nomination. Triumphant but exhausted, Roosevelt believed that Wilson would reward him with a federal job.

Meanwhile, he had to run again for state senator. It seemed likely then he would easily be reelected, but in August, as the campaign began, he developed typhoid fever after drinking some contaminated water. In bed for weeks, he stared at the walls and worried. He needed help, but from whom and how?

At that point Roosevelt hired an unlikely helper, a reporter, Louis McHenry Howe, he had met while Howe was covering the legislature for a newspaper. Howe was physically unimpressive—only 5 feet tall, extremely scrawny, often wearing seedy and shabby suits. He had failed to make a living in journalism and often needed money from his mother-in-law to support his family. But Howe was something of a political genius, and he deeply admired and respected Roosevelt. He believed Roosevelt was headed for the White House long before anyone else even thought that the young man had a future.

While Roosevelt was bed-bound, Howe managed a brilliant campaign, using newspaper advertisements and personal letters to voters to win support for Roosevelt. He traveled the district to whip up enthusiasm for his candidate. As a result, Roosevelt won on Election Day, although by only a plurality, not a majority. Roosevelt was deeply grateful, and from then on, Howe served as his chief aide.

4

"He was young . . . and made some mistakes"

In spite of his reelection as a New York state senator, Roosevelt's career in Albany was about to end. Woodrow Wilson was elected president in 1912 and wanted to reward his staunch supporter Roosevelt with a new job. In particular, Roosevelt had his eye on the post of assistant secretary of the navy, the job that had catapulted Theodore Roosevelt into the White House. The position was offered to Franklin Roosevelt by the new secretary of the navy, Josephus Daniels.

The two men seemed like opposites. On the one hand, Roosevelt was only thirty-one years old and a product of East Coast aristocracy and the finest schools. Full of boundless energy, Roosevelt was eager for action. Although he had never served in the Navy, his lifelong hobby had been ships, sailing, and naval history, and at long last he could try out his ideas. He advocated big government spending to build up the strength and power of the Navy.

On the other hand there was Daniels, almost twenty years older than Roosevelt and the former editor and publisher of a Raleigh, North Carolina newspaper. Daniels could be firm and stubborn but gave the impression of being a humble and easygoing country bumpkin. He knew something about naval affairs because of family members who had served in the Navy. But he was a pacifist and believed in preventing wars, not in gearing up to fight them.

Roosevelt gloried in the ceremonies and medals of the Navy and eagerly befriended admirals and top brass. He often ordered up ships for his personal use—to pick up his family at Campobello, for example, and deliver them to Hyde Park. He coached Eleanor and their young children in what to do when they went aboard a battleship, whom to shake hands with, and how to salute the flag.

Daniels, on the other hand, viewed all Navy men alike and often offended officers by addressing lowly sailors as "young gentlemen" and by setting up programs to educate enlisted men.

At first, the heavy paperwork in his new job overwhelmed Roosevelt. He wrote to his mother: "I am baptized, confirmed, sworn in, vaccinated—and somewhat at sea! For over an hour I have been signing papers which had to be accepted on faith—but I hope luck will keep me out of jail."[1] Roosevelt had two assistants—Charles McCarthy, who had worked for other assistant secretaries, and Louis Howe, whom Roosevelt brought with him. Later he also hired a former friend from Harvard, Livingston Davis.

Daniels treated Roosevelt in a kind and fatherly way, even when Roosevelt rebelled and contradicted him. Once, when Daniels went on a two-day trip, he left Roosevelt in charge. He returned to find that Roosevelt had told newspaper reporters, "You remember what happened the last time a Roosevelt occupied a similar position?"[2] The comment referred to the time when Theodore Roosevelt had been serving as acting secretary of the navy and had ordered Commodore Dewey to sail into Manila Bay in the Philippines. The incident touched off the Spanish-American War. Teddy had directly contradicted orders left behind by the secretary of the navy, but his flamboyance and take-charge attitude so impressed Americans that he later ended up as president.

Franklin viewed himself as the same type of person. He did not like taking orders, and in fact his Navy job was the last one in which he was number two to someone else. His parents had raised him to believe he was a special person, part of a special class. That was the attitude he brought to Washington, D.C.

Soon Franklin Roosevelt was involved in some international incidents very similar to those that Theodore Roosevelt had faced. Although Franklin had some of the same nationalistic, militaristic ideas that Uncle Teddy favored, the results were not as explosive. Daniels and Woodrow Wilson remained in control of the situation and of Franklin Roosevelt.

In 1913 Army and Navy officers feared that Japan might attack some U.S. naval ships stationed in China. They urged that the ships be moved to the Philippines, but Daniels and Woodrow Wilson feared that the ship movement might touch off war with Japan. Roosevelt supported the admirals' point of view, but publicly he backed Daniels and Wilson.

A year later a similar incident came up when Wilson, who had refused to recognize the regime of a new Mexican president, Victoriano Huerta, ordered U.S. battleships to sail to Mexico.

Roosevelt, touring the West Coast, began making militant speeches in support of Wilson and plunged into efforts to get troops ready on the West Coast in case they should have to sail to Mexico, too. "We're not looking for trouble, but we're ready for anything," he told reporters.[3]

But other South American nations offered to mediate the dispute between Huerta and Wilson, and Wilson accepted. Even after he heard about the peacemaking efforts, Roosevelt kept up the warlike speeches. But when he returned to Washington, D.C., Daniels only scolded him gently. "He was young then and made some mistakes," Daniels later said.[4]

While in Washington, Roosevelt kept in touch with New York State politics. In fact, in 1914, he decided to run for U.S. senator from New York in the primary. It was the first time that voters in New York themselves, and not the parties, could decide who the Republican and Democratic candidates would be.

It proved a poor time to run. Roosevelt was worn out by the long hours of his Navy job and campaigned very little. Meanwhile, Tammany Hall chose a decent and respectable candidate, James Gerard, the U.S. ambassador to Germany, and the Wilson administration did not want to back Roosevelt and thus alienate the Tammany machine. Roosevelt suffered a crushing defeat—he polled only 76,888 votes compared with 210,765 for Gerard. Gerard later lost to the Republican candidate. Gradually, Roosevelt was finding out that if his career was to move forward, he had to make peace with Tammany Hall.

One reason why Roosevelt had campaigned so little was the growing political crisis in Europe. During the summer, Austria and Germany had declared war on the tiny Balkan nation of Serbia. Russia, France, and England had declared war in turn on Austria and Germany.

Rushing to his office from Campobello after he heard the news, Roosevelt was upset at how casually officials in Washington viewed the situation. Most Americans believed that the European war would end very quickly and would probably not involve them. Roosevelt disagreed and concluded that the Wilson administration was totally unprepared. "A complete smash-up is inevitable," he wrote to Eleanor, "and there are a great many problems for us to consider. Mr. D. [Josephus Daniels] totally fails to grasp the situation."[5]

Americans debated whether the United States should take sides in the war or remain neutral. One group of U.S.

senators favored intervention, but Secretary of State William Jennings Bryan, Woodrow Wilson, and Josephus Daniels opposed it. Wilson favored the Allies—Britain, France and Russia—but he did not want war.

Almost excited about the prospect of war, Roosevelt pushed the administration to prepare for the worst by building ships and weapons. He wrote to Eleanor in early August telling her that he had been up till 3 A.M. working for three days in a row. "I feel hurt," he told her, "because the Emperor William [Kaiser Wilhelm of Germany] has left the U.S. out—he has declared war against everybody else."[6]

At times he seemed almost uncaring about what war might cost in human lives. "In time of war would we be content like the turtle to withdraw into our own shell and see an enemy supersede us in every outlying part, usurp our commerce and destroy our influence as a nation throughout the world?" he asked in a magazine article.[7]

Often Roosevelt seemed to side with Wilson's enemies—prowar advocates like Senator Henry Cabot Lodge and Representative Augustus P. Gardner, both Republicans from Massachusetts. Gardner, for example, made a speech charging that U.S. forces were ill prepared for war. Soon after, Roosevelt issued a long memo to the press supporting Gardner's claim that the Navy was short of men and ships. In doing so, Roosevelt directly contradicted Josephus Daniels, who was out of town at the time. "The enclosed is the truth and even if it gets me into trouble I am perfectly ready to stand by it," Roosevelt wrote to his wife.[8]

Sometimes Roosevelt half-jokingly told admirals who were frustrated with Daniels to come back to see him on a day when Daniels was out of town.

Why didn't Daniels fire this young firebrand who often embarrassed him and showed a general lack of respect for his boss? And why didn't Woodrow Wilson demand the resignation of this underling who contradicted his higher-ups?

In spite of his rebelliousness, Roosevelt could still charm and impress his superiors. And in spite of his disagreements with Woodrow Wilson's policies, he still respected his bosses. "I have worked very gladly under Mr. Daniels and I wish the public could realize how much he has done for the Navy," he wrote to one supporter in 1916.[9]

Although Wilson wanted to keep the United States out of the war, Germany seemed intent on provoking her. Time and again, German U-boats, or submarines, torpedoed civilian passenger liners and freighters on the high seas. On May 7, 1914, a German sub sunk the *Lusitania,* a huge British ocean liner, in the Irish Sea. Nearly 1,200 people died, 128 of them American. Americans were horrified; did this mean that innocent civilians of a neutral country could no longer travel where they wished? The Germans claimed the *Lusitania* was carrying thousands of cases of cartridges and shrapnel shells for the Allies.

President Wilson protested sharply to the Germans; he demanded that the submarine warfare end or the United States would hold Germany accountable. William Jennings Bryan, believing that Wilson was giving the Germans an ultimatum which would lead to war, reacted by resigning as secretary of state. Roosevelt, of course, supported Wilson's new stand.

As the months passed, the submarine warfare continued and Wilson sent more letters of protest. At times the Germans seemed to back down, but they also pressured the United States to get Britain to stop shipping ammunition on civilian vessels.

Amid this growing crisis, Wilson faced a reelection race in 1916. His Republican opponent was Charles Evans Hughes, former governor of New York and former associate justice of the U.S. Supreme Court. At first it appeared that Hughes—who had the backing of the former president, Theodore Roosevelt—might win. But he was a poor campaigner. In addition, the nation was swayed by Wilson's campaign slogan: "He kept us out of war." Wilson eventually won, though by a narrow margin—277 electoral votes to 254 for Hughes.

Trying to make peace, Wilson offered to be a mediator in the war between Germany and the Allied nations. He also proposed forming a league of nations to work to prevent future similar wars. Both sides rebuffed him, and a group of senators opposed his proposal for an international league.

Then, early in 1917, Germany began unrestricted submarine warfare again. In mid-March German subs torpedoed three American ships. Soon, the Cabinet, including the pacifist Daniels, was advising Wilson that the end had come.

On April 2, Wilson appeared before a special session of Congress. Franklin and Eleanor Roosevelt sat in the audience as a very serious and worried President Wilson urged Congress to declare war. "The world must be made safe for democracy," Wilson said.[10] As he ended his speech, the senators and congressmen rose to their feet to cheer and wave tiny American flags.

Roosevelt threw himself into preparing the Navy for war, working longer and harder than ever. World War I brought sweeping growth in the size and complexity of the federal government, and he was right in the middle, learning how government operates in a crisis.

Throughout his time in Washington, D.C., he had had several minor illnesses, colds and flu primarily. This continued to be the case. But to those around him, he seemed vigorous and energetic. In his mid-thirties, he was handsome and admired by office secretaries and Washington hostesses. One newspaper wrote: "His face is long, firmly shaped and set with marks of confidence. There are faint wrinkles on a high straight forehead. Intensely blue eyes rest in light shadow. A firm, thin mouth breaks quickly to laugh, openly and freely.''[11]

His first plan was to resign his job and enlist for active service. His now aging cousin Theodore urged him to get into uniform, but Wilson and Daniels discouraged Franklin from joining up. So did the admirals and generals who depended on him to present their views to Wilson.

Still impatient with Daniels, Franklin pushed to speed up the building of destroyers and submarines. Some of his complaints about Daniels were leaked to the press, and the *Wall Street Journal* complained that the only person getting things done in the Navy Department was Franklin Roosevelt.

Perhaps Roosevelt's most unique idea during World War I was his proposal for laying a barrier of mines and nets across the entrance to the North Sea, to make it harder for German submarines to get out into the North Atlantic to attack Allied ships. Other military men had had the same idea, but Roosevelt pushed for it the most. Roosevelt liked to think that the net filled with 70,000 mines played a role in ending the war sooner, but probably it was installed too late to have much effect.

Although Roosevelt never wore a uniform, he did persuade Wilson and Daniels to send him to France in the summer of 1918 to inspect Allied forces. In July he and his aide, Livingston Davis, sailed on a new destroyer, the U.S.S. *Dyer*.

The ocean voyage was fairly uneventful except for rough seas, but in later years Roosevelt made it sound as if the *Dyer* had nearly been attacked by German submarines. Roosevelt stopped first in England to meet British officials and the king of England. He also spent time with the millionaire Astor family at their English country estate.

Then he went on to war-torn France. Although military officials often found him quarters in comfortable homes and hotels and fed him the best of meals, he insisted on visiting the battlefields of Belleau Wood and Verdun and other areas. No major battles were being fought, but he picked his way around trenches and barbed wire and through the bombed-out farms and homes. He heard the whistle and thunder of nearby enemy guns. He smelled the decaying corpses of horses and saw the crosses marking the graves of French, American, and German soldiers.

Sometimes his letters home sounded as if he and his hard-drinking companion Davis were at a resort as he wrote about the "splendid entertainment" by an enlisted men's jazz band at one French town or about a "hop" in a seaplane that gave him "an excellent idea of the geography in this region." [12] But he took his mission seriously and often told the soldiers that he wished he could be in uniform rather than tied to a desk job.

When he left France, he was sick with Spanish influenza, a deadly disease sweeping Europe. When he reached New York on September 19, he had to be taken ashore on a stretcher and was away from his job for a month. While ill, he drafted a report for Josephus Daniels about his adventures. He still hoped to go back to Europe in the military, but it was not to be. On November 11, 1918, an armistice was signed. After four years the war had finally ended.

At home, another crisis had developed, one that threatened to destroy his marriage and possibly his career. Roosevelt had secretly fallen in love with Lucy Page Mercer, a twenty-six-year-old woman whom Eleanor had hired in 1913 to serve as her social secretary—to send letters and invitations and make appointments. But Lucy was more than that and almost became a member of the Roosevelt family. Often, while Franklin Roosevelt was in Washington, Eleanor and the children traveled to Campobello or Hyde Park for long visits, leaving him alone with Lucy.

Then, while Franklin was ill after his trip to Europe, Eleanor found love letters that Lucy had written to him during his trip. Eleanor was crushed. All her life the people she loved had mistreated her, and suddenly the one man she had trusted had betrayed her as well. She had devoted herself selflessly to Franklin, but he had rejected her for a younger, prettier woman.

What followed is shrouded in mystery, but some family members say that Eleanor offered to step aside so that Franklin could marry Lucy. But the lovers rejected the idea. Lucy, a Catholic, did not want to marry a divorced man, and Franklin did not want to leave his children. But probably more important was his fear that if he left Eleanor he would destroy his political career. Married politicians of that era could have romances with women other than their wives, but they could not divorce their wives and be elected.

So Lucy and Franklin parted ways, and Eleanor stayed with Franklin. Over the next few months the Roosevelts treated each other very carefully, working to please each other. Franklin tried to share more of his work and ideas with Eleanor, and Eleanor tried to attend more of the parties that Franklin enjoyed so much. But their marriage had changed forever. Eleanor would no longer focus all her attention on Franklin and his career. Gradually, she built new interests outside their home, but her emotional scars never healed completely.

5

"I do not feel in the least bit downhearted"

What Woodrow Wilson had called the war to end all wars finally ended on November 11, 1918, after 10 million people had died. Early in 1919 peace talks began in Paris. But although the guns fell silent, political unrest had not ended.

President Wilson had listed for the world his program of Fourteen Points that could help build a firm peace after the war. The first few were general ideas calling for such things as open treaties to be openly arrived at, freedom of the seas, and removal of trade barriers. Then there were specific points calling for changes in European borders and creation of a free Poland. The Fourteenth Point was the most important to him—it called for forming a general association of nations, or League of Nations, to keep the peace in the future. Wilson had also sworn that Germany would not be severely punished for its role in the war.

In January 1919 Wilson went to the Paris peace talks. Roosevelt and Eleanor went to Europe as well, but Roosevelt's job was to make decisions about Navy property that had to be sold or returned to the United States. He knew nothing about what went on in the peace talks, nor did almost anyone else. The negotiations were shrouded in secrecy; Wilson had brought very few advisers with him. Germany had no representatives at the talks. What the public did know was that Wilson was intent on getting his League of Nations written into the peace treaty.

While on their trip, Roosevelt and Eleanor learned that Theodore Roosevelt had died in his sleep of a blood clot on the lung. Both of them were shocked.

Cheering crowds greeted Wilson when he returned home briefly in February to update the nation on the peace talks. He was confident that the Senate would approve the treaty even though the Republicans controlled Congress and his old enemy, Senator Henry Cabot Lodge, opposed the proposed Covenant of the League of Nations. What Lodge and others disliked was a provision in the covenant that the United States would send troops to defend member nations. Lodge contended that a peace treaty with Germany should be signed before the League was set up.

Wilson insisted that there could be no real peace without the League and then headed back to Paris. While there, he suffered a minor stroke and his ability to handle the crisis seemed impaired. Again and again, he had to compromise on his Fourteen Points to keep his precious League of Nations in the treaty. The treaty being drawn up ordered Germany to pay heavily for damages suffered by civilians during the war. Her armed forces were reduced; she also lost many territories. When the final draft of the treaty was revealed on May 7, many of Wilson's supporters felt angry and betrayed. They believed that the burden that Germany was forced to bear would cause economic chaos in Europe. The Germans felt Wilson had tricked them.

Wilson embarked on a cross-country trip to campaign for the treaty and League of Nations. Along the way he had a more serious stroke and had to return to the White House. Fellow Democrats urged him to compromise with Senator Lodge and other opponents, but Wilson, lying ill in bed, refused to make changes. The running of the United States had been taken over by Wilson's wife, secretary, and doctor. Ultimately, the treaty failed to win Senate approval. Technically, the United States remained at war with Germany and the Central Powers, although the fighting had long since ended. Peace resolutions to officially end the war were not adopted until July 1921.

Clearly, Wilson was falling from favor, and Roosevelt, who had previously supported the League, wanted to distance himself from the administration. He had to build a political future apart from Wilson and Secretary of the Navy Daniels. One of the Navy's admirals was pushing Congress to launch an investigation of the Navy Department, and in particular Daniels. Roosevelt feared that he might get caught up in the controversy. In what many regarded as a callous betrayal of his boss, he made a speech in Brooklyn in early 1920 in which he declared that in order to push Daniels to prepare for war "I committed enough illegal acts to put me in jail for 999 years."[1]

Among other actions he had taken, Roosevelt said, he had ordered thousands of dollars' worth of guns without the permission of Daniels or Wilson just before the war began.

Daniels was outraged; much of what Roosevelt had said was an exaggeration. Even many of Roosevelt's friends thought he had gone too far. For a while, Daniels considered firing Roosevelt; but the administration was in such upheaval due to Wilson's illness that Daniels decided it would add to the confusion if Roosevelt left. Almost immediately, Roosevelt was sorry for giving the speech and tried to explain to the press why he had said what he said.

As the summer of 1920 approached, Republicans and Democrats debated whom they would nominate for the presidency. In June the Republicans chose Warren Harding, a man who promised an end to the idealistic but also impractical course set by Wilson and pledged to return to peace and normalcy.

Despite being unable to think or speak clearly, Wilson thought about seeking a third term. The Democrats, however, wanted a new leader to offer to the American people.

The Democratic convention opened on July 28, 1920, in San Francisco. As usual, Roosevelt plunged eagerly into the convention hubbub, where he charmed almost everyone he met. He was the picture of activity, leaping over chairs, running here and there to talk to delegates.

The Democrats had hoped to nominate Herbert Hoover, a wealthy engineer who had earned acclaim for managing the nation's food supplies during the war. Many prominent Democrats also thought that Franklin Roosevelt, despite his problems with Wilson and Daniels, would make a great vice presidential candidate with Hoover.

Roosevelt was optimistic about his chances and even drew up some proposals that he hoped the national convention would write into its platform: new federal loans for farmers and home builders, reorganization of the nation's railroads, and more federal aid for highways. As early as 1919 Roosevelt had foreseen the growing division between the Republican and Democratic parties. The Republicans represented special privilege, conservatism and destruction, he contended in a speech given to the Democratic National Committee. The Democrats, he said, represented liberalism, idealism, and progress.

But eventually, Hoover backed out of the proposal to run with Roosevelt and decided to work with the Republicans instead.

In San Francisco, the Democratic convention was deadlocked for a long time, with no candidate able to get the two-thirds vote needed. Finally Ohio's governor, James M. Cox, a progressive candidate, won out. Cox knew almost nothing about Roosevelt, but he and other Democrats quickly agreed that Roosevelt would make the ideal vice president. Roosevelt was young and had a well known name; he was from New York, which meant he would balance the ticket geographically. Even Tammany Hall was not opposed. Tammany boss Charles Murphy told Cox: "This young Roosevelt is no good, but if you want him, go ahead and we'll vote for him."[2]

Roosevelt, who had not enjoyed taking orders in the Navy Department, had some reservations about being number two to a president. But he was convinced that he could turn the vice presidency into a "highly respected and live-wire office."[3]

When Roosevelt arrived in Hyde Park after the convention, hundreds of townspeople waving flags waited outside the gates of his family estate. On the porch his mother hugged him and told him how proud she was. She had not been at the convention and neither had Eleanor, who had had no idea that her husband would be nominated. But Eleanor rushed back from Campobello and joined Roosevelt for a celebration in Dayton, Ohio, where Governor Cox gave a formal acceptance speech. As the campaign began, Roosevelt pledged to reorganize the government and continue involvement of the United States in the world's problems. He predicted that Wilson's dream of forming a League of Nations would one day come true. "The League will not die," he told a crowd of 5,000 people milling on the lawn of his home. "An idea does not die which meets the call of the hearts of our mothers."[4]

Almost immediately, the national spotlight focused on the Roosevelt family. Newsreel and newspaper cameramen seemed to follow them everywhere—to Hyde Park, to Campobello. Even Roosevelt's mother was interviewed for an article in *Good Housekeeping* titled "My Boy Franklin by Sara Delano Roosevelt."

In early August, Roosevelt boarded a train on the first of three long speaking tours to campaign for the Democratic ticket. Appearing in almost every state outside of the South, he gave thousands of speeches and talks and met hundreds of important Democrats. He and Louis Howe jotted down the names of many of these people for future contacts. They were already thinking ahead to the future. They believed that if Cox could not win in 1920, Roosevelt might run for governor of New York in 1922 or the Democratic party might choose Roosevelt as its presidential nominee in 1924.

Everywhere he went, large crowds turned out to hear him and many were impressed by his winning smile, college boy good looks, and clear, strong voice. But Roosevelt and his staff also found the crowds uninterested in the League of Nations and bitter toward Woodrow Wilson. Even the optimistic Roosevelt sensed that he could not overcome the anti-Wilson feeling with charm alone.

Eleanor Roosevelt began the campaign feeling shy and out of place but soon joined in the excitement. She no longer wanted to simply sit at home and tend her children. Besides, it was the first national election in which women could vote and it seemed like a good time for a woman to get involved. So Eleanor joined her husband for his second Western campaign tour and traveled with him for three weeks.

Along the way she developed a new respect for and friendship with Louis Howe, Roosevelt's campaign aide. Howe had always admired her and thought she had unique intelligence and abilities, even though Eleanor and Sara Roosevelt had always looked down on him. Howe set aside time to explain to Eleanor what was going on. He discussed campaign issues and newspaper coverage with her. He showed her drafts of Roosevelt's speeches.

Eleanor learned how to sit and listen to the same speech over and over again while looking excited and attentive. She learned to greet total strangers as if they were her best friends. Eleanor wrote to her mother-in-law: "It is becoming almost impossible to stop F. now when he begins to speak, 10 minutes is always 20, 30 is always 45 & the evening speeches are now about 2 hours! The men all get out & wave at him in front & when nothing succeeds I yank his coat tails!"[5]

When Election Day arrived, the chances for the Cox-Roosevelt ticket seemed very slim, largely because of the lack of public support for Woodrow Wilson and the League of Nations.

On a cold, rainy day in Hyde Park, Roosevelt, Eleanor, and Sara cast their votes. And the election results matched the dismal dreariness of the weather for Roosevelt. Harding and Coolidge carried thirty-seven states and 404 of the 531 electoral votes in a tremendous Republican landslide. The Democrats did not win any seats outside of the Deep South; Roosevelt had not even been able to carry his own state, New York, and all Democrats running for state office in New York had lost.

Outwardly, Roosevelt remained enthusiastic and cheerful, although the crushing loss must have hurt. "I do not feel in the least bit down-hearted," he told a friend. "It seems to me that everything possible was done during the campaign, and no other course would have been honorable or successful. As long as the other people were going to win, I am glad they had such a clear majority." [6]

At any rate, he had made a name for himself—apart from his connection to Uncle Teddy Roosevelt. He had won new friends in the Democratic party and had built a foundation for his political future. But next time, he had already decided, he wanted his name at the top of the ticket, not as number two.

In early 1921, out of politics for what he thought would be a brief period, he set to work to make money for his family. He formed a law firm in New York City with two friends, Langdon Marvin and Grenville T. Emmet. But he also accepted a post as vice president in the New York offices of the Fidelity and Deposit Company of Maryland, a surety bonding company. The company believed that just having the Roosevelt name and personality at their disposal would draw in enough clients to make him worth his salary of $25,000 a year, five times his Navy Department pay. Louis Howe went along to serve as Roosevelt's special assistant at Fidelity and Deposit.

While Roosevelt sought contracts and new business for his firm, Eleanor got more involved with politics. She joined the board of the League of Women Voters and was a delegate to the national League convention.

As Roosevelt built his new business career, it was a time of major changes in the U.S. economy. A brief but fairly severe depression took place. Prices for farm products were dropping, and many farmers were leaving their land for the cities. More and more people were working in offices and factories. Large corporations grew larger and had a strong voice in the new Harding administration. Graft and corruption seemed rampant as companies and lobbyists bought influence with politicians.

During the summer of 1921 Roosevelt was also occupied with a continued Senate investigation of some of the affairs of the Navy Department. He was out of public office, but he was worried that any hint of scandal might cast a shadow on his hopes for his future.

While Roosevelt had been in the Navy Department, heavy drinking, drug use, and other illicit activities among sailors had been reported at the Newport, Rhode Island, naval station. Roosevelt had authorized an investigation, but his investigators got carried away with their job. Sailors had been used as decoys to entice and entrap other sailors and in some cases had committed illegal acts as part of the investigation. The Senate subcommittee contended that Roosevelt's actions had been "a most deplorably, disgraceful and unnatural proceeding."[7]

Roosevelt was at Campobello in mid-July when he heard about the committee report about to be released. He rushed to Washington and demanded a chance to appear before the investigating subcommittee. The subcommittee gave him only eight hours to look over 6,000 pages of testimony before giving them his reply. While Washington, D.C., sweltered through a heat wave, he worked furiously on his rebuttal statement.

Appearing before the subcommittee, he told the senators that as soon as he had heard details of the Newport investigation, he had ordered immediately that it stop. He accused the Republican senators on the committee of playing politics and of attacking him unfairly to gain a political advantage.

Huge newspaper headlines carried the story of the affair and gave only little play to Roosevelt's denials. He was exhausted and crushed by the ordeal even though reporters quickly dropped the story. Roosevelt was out of office and the press was no longer interested in the alleged misdeeds of the former administration.

His family was anxious for him to return to Canada to spend the summer with them. But instead of returning immediately to Campobello, he spent two weeks in New York to clean up business at his office. On July 28, he also took a fateful trip with other dignitaries to a new Boy Scout camp at Bear Mountain in New York. It was a rollicking and fun-filled day with parades and speeches and a campfire where Roosevelt spoke to the cheering boys. But it is believed that somewhere that day he inhaled or ingested a virus that would change his life forever.

6

"Below his waist he cannot move at all"

After the long, trying summer of 1921, Roosevelt was looking forward to returning to Campobello to unwind and relax. But over the next few days, he seemed unable to slow down his hectic pace.

Instead of going by train to Campobello, Roosevelt sailed there on the *Sabalo,* a steam-powered yacht owned by Van Lear Black, head of Fidelity and Deposit. What should have been a leisurely trip turned into a harrowing voyage in rough, foggy seas off Maine. Roosevelt took over the wheel of the boat from the captain, who was unfamiliar with the rocky coastline. On August 7 the group finally arrived to find the Roosevelt and Howe families waiting on the dock.

Summers at Campobello were always crammed with lots of activity. Although Roosevelt felt strangely tired, the very next day he went off with Black and his friends to fish on the Bay of Fundy. Sometime that afternoon, while baiting hooks for his guests and running back and forth on the boat, he fell overboard. "The water was so cold it seemed paralyzing," he said later.[1]

The chill he felt was a warning of what was to come, but it did not slow him down. Roosevelt still felt tired and achy that evening and the next morning as well when Van Lear Black and his party sailed away. On Wednesday, August 10, he felt worse, but the weather was beautiful and his children wanted an outing. After lunch he took Eleanor, James, and Elliott for a long sail on the family sloop, the *Vireo*. Nearing home, they spotted a tiny forest fire on a small island and went ashore to beat out the flames with evergreen boughs. The hot, dirty work made them feel grimy and smoky. Once back at Campobello, they didn't rest even though it was four o'clock. Roosevelt proposed that they take a quick swim to cool off. They raced on foot to Lake Glen Severn, a small and warm freshwater pond on the other side of the island. After their swim, Roosevelt took a quick dip in the icy Bay of Fundy. But as he dried off later, he failed to feel the bracing glow that usually came over him.

Back at the cottage, he sat down on the porch in his wet bathing suit to read his mail. He was too tired to change his clothes. He went to bed early and took dinner on a tray in his room. The next morning he woke up and found that his legs almost collapsed under him as he walked toward the bathroom. He quickly returned to bed; his temperature measured 102 degrees. Eleanor was growing worried. She sent the children off on a camping trip and called in the summer doctor from nearby Lubec. The physician, E. H. Bennet, was puzzled by Roosevelt's symptoms but decided that his patient had no more than a very bad cold.

But Roosevelt knew it was worse than that. Just a cold could not weaken his muscles the way this illness did. By the next day, he could no longer stand up alone to go to the bathroom. His temperature inched upward, and his legs felt numb and dead. Even his skin seemed to be on fire. He could not stand the pressure of a sheet or blanket on his skin. Even the breezes that blew in the window were painful to him.

Increasingly worried, Louis Howe and Dr. Bennet went out in a boat, traveling up and down the summer resorts to find a doctor who could give them another opinion. They found Dr. W. W. Keen of Philadelphia staying at a Bar Harbor resort, and he agreed to drive up to the cottage for the night. "He thinks a clot of blood from a sudden congestion has settled in the lower spinal cord temporarily removing the power to move though not to feel," Eleanor wrote to Franklin's half brother, James, on August 14.[2]

Dr. Keen also advised that a masseur be hired and that Eleanor begin massaging Roosevelt's legs immediately. But the massage only added to Roosevelt's pain. Hour after hour, Howe and Eleanor took turns nursing Roosevelt and caught an hour or two of sleep here and there.

Roosevelt grew more deeply depressed as the paralysis spread into his back. Soon he could not even sit up in bed or take care of the simplest bodily functions. On August 14 and 15 he hovered near death.

Then his temperature began to fall. The crisis of the illness had past, and his spirits began to rise again. But Eleanor already sensed that a terrible struggle still lay ahead. Dr. Keen had revised his diagnosis and said that Roosevelt might have a lesion in his spinal cord that could cause serious future problems. "I dread the time when I have to tell Franklin and it wrings my heart for it is all so much worse to a man than to a woman," she wrote to James.[3]

Louis Howe was greatly dissatisfied by Keen's diagnosis and wrote long letters to Franklin's uncle Fred Delano, describing his nephew's symptoms. Specialists in Boston told Delano they believed that Roosevelt had poliomyelitis, or infantile paralysis as it was often called because it most commonly attacked children and young adults.

Since the 1960s millions have been protected with the polio vaccine. But during the early twentieth century several epidemics of this virus swept through the United States. Once ingested via the throat, the virus passes through the blood and lymph systems and can eventually invade the spinal cord.

The first symptoms of polio are headache, fever, nausea, and a sore throat—much as Roosevelt experienced. But more than 80 percent of those who develop the disease recover in a few days with no lasting effects. For them, having polio is like having a bad cold.

But those whose immunity to disease is low, as Roosevelt's may have been due to work and stress, can get much sicker. Many medical experts believe that because Roosevelt spent his childhood with almost no contact with other children, he may have been more susceptible to polio. Lack of regular exposure to childhood diseases meant that he built up very little immunity and developed illnesses later in life that most people have as children.

Her fear growing, Eleanor arranged for a leading authority on poliomyelitis, Dr. Robert Williamson Lovett of Boston, to visit Campobello. On August 25 he confirmed that Roosevelt had the dreaded disease.

Eleanor was afraid for the children, but Dr. Lovett said that if they were going to get the disease, they would have already done so. He also advised her to stop massaging Roosevelt's legs immediately; it would only damage his muscles more. He told the family to expect Roosevelt to be very depressed about his condition. But he had some encouraging words, too. He believed that Roosevelt did not have one of the severest types of polio and that he might actually regain full or partial use of some of his muscles.

Inside the spinal cord the polio virus can destroy the motor nerve cells that send signals from the brain to the muscles. Cells that are destroyed cannot grow back; however, those that are only partly damaged can gradually recover their normal use.

Except for giving Roosevelt hot baths, Dr. Lovett advised, little else could be done for a while except to wait and see what would happen. Roosevelt was very calm and quiet after hearing the news, but Eleanor could read the strain etched on his face. All he could do was sit in bed and wait hour after hour to find out if he would walk again, or if he could even sit up again.

As his doctor wrote at the time: "He has such courage, such ambition, and yet at the same time, such an extraordinarily sensitive emotional mechanism that it will take all the skill which we can muster to lead him successfully to a recognition of what he really faces without crushing him." [4]

The next crisis involved Franklin's mother, who was in Europe that summer and knew nothing about her son's illness. Eleanor had not wanted to write her about it or Sara would have spent her sea voyage home worrying.

Usually when Sara's boat arrived, Roosevelt stood on the dock to greet her. But this time, Eleanor sent Franklin's half brother, James, to break the news to Sara. Sara was shocked and devastated and immediately headed for Campobello.

She arrived to find Roosevelt still in bed and gravely ill but trying hard for her sake to pretend that nothing was seriously wrong, as he had even as a small child. Sara wrote later to her brother Fred: "Below his waist he cannot move at all. His legs . . . have to be moved often as they ache when long in one position. He and Eleanor decided at once to be cheerful and the atmosphere of the house is all happiness . . . Dr. Bennet just came and said, 'This boy is going to get well all right.' They went into his room and I can hear them all laughing. Eleanor in the lead." [5]

In spite of her brave front, Sara concluded that her son's career and public life were over. It had been fine while it lasted, she believed, but as an invalid he must retire to Hyde Park to lead a quiet life as a country gentleman. He could return to his hobbies of birds, forestry, and naval prints and stamp collecting. She had never completely approved of his political career, and while it was devastating that he might never walk again, the one good thing about his paralysis was that he would no longer campaign and mix with the masses. He could spend more time with her and with his family.

Eleanor and Louis Howe felt differently, and very soon they began to clash with Roosevelt's mother on this subject.

By mid-September, the Roosevelts had decided to take Franklin back to New York City. The trip was painful and humiliating. He was taken by stretcher and luggage cart to a special railroad car that his uncle Fred Delano had hired to carry him down the East Coast. He was still feverish, and every bump and jolt along the way made his back and legs throb.

All this was done quietly and with little public notice. When newspaper reporters finally spotted Roosevelt, he was sitting up in his train berth and jauntily smoking a cigarette.

For some time Louis Howe had kept the press from finding out what was really wrong with Roosevelt, although reporters knew he had been ill. But finally, when Roosevelt returned to New York City to enter Presbyterian Hospital as a patient, they were told he had had polio. But still they did not get all the details. Their stories said that Roosevelt had lost use of his legs below the knees for a month, but that his doctor said he would not be crippled or permanently disabled. Throughout his life, Roosevelt and Howe tried to keep from the public exactly how damaging his illness had been.

The problem was that handicapped people in the 1920s were viewed with shame and embarrassment. If they were not locked up permanently in hospitals, they were hidden away in their homes. Public schools turned them away, and few hospitals had programs to teach them skills for coping with their disabilities. For Roosevelt to admit publicly that he would never walk again on his own could have destroyed his political career.

At the time of his return to New York City, Roosevelt also believed that eventually he would walk again. But George Draper, the doctor who took over his case in the city, was very depressed about his patient. Roosevelt's legs were totally paralyzed, he could not sit up on his own without support, his arm muscles were like jelly. He was still in pain and at times ran a fever. But those who visited him were amazed at how he cheerfully insisted that one day he would walk again. The old courage and enthusiasm that had carried him through so many past crises were returning. "I have been given every reason to expect that my somewhat rebellious legs will permit me to join in another course of training sometime in the future," he wrote to Yale football coach Walter Camp, who had once led a physical fitness course for Navy Department executives like Roosevelt.[6]

On October 28, 1921, Roosevelt finally went home from the hospital. By then he could swing himself into a wheelchair by a strap hung from the ceiling. But his doctors believed that gradually he must face the fact that he would never walk by himself again.

The Roosevelts found themselves cramped and crowded into their New York City town house, the one adjoining Sara Roosevelt's house. Room had to be found for a trained nurse and also for Louis Howe, who wanted to remain close by while Roosevelt convalesced. Eleanor had to sleep on a bed in one of the children's rooms. Daughter Anna had to be moved out of her room.

Eleanor struggled with the constant nursing that Roosevelt required and with fighting off Sara, who complained constantly about her son's care and objected strongly to Louis Howe's living with the Roosevelts.

By Christmas, Roosevelt was more active, crawling on the floor while dragging his useless legs behind him, Indian wrestling with his sons. His arm and upper-trunk muscles returned to normal strength. His back and stomach muscles were improving. But then in January 1922 the weakened muscles in his legs atrophied and contracted, and his legs bent back in horrible contortions. The doctors put his legs into thick plaster casts, and every day had to drive a wedge in behind the knee to stretch his tendons. Roosevelt bore the painful torture patiently with a smile. The man whom many had believed was a spoiled rich boy was proving to have courage and determination in the face of suffering and despair.

He tried to put others at ease about his physical condition. At first his children were embarrassed and uncomfortable about his handicaps. So he threw back the covers on the bed to show them his withered legs while he pointed out each muscle and how it was supposed to work. "How we loved to talk about father's gluteus maximus!" said son James. "He would work to wiggle one toe, straining and sweating. He never succeeded, but he believed he did. He reported to us the return of feeling and we cheered as though hearing of advances by our side in a football game."[7]

He dropped out of his chair at dinner and crawled around the table to show guests he was still agile and strong. He inched up and down the four-story staircase of the Manhattan town house.

But he was also determined to find a cure for his legs, and he wrote to polio patients and doctors around the country. He tried massage, special baths and exercises underwater, horseback riding, and treatment with electric currents.

Many people have speculated that his illness was a purifying fire for him—that it caused him to look inward for the first time in his life, to realize for the first time what it meant to suffer misfortune through no fault of his own. As a consequence, they say, he was better able to understand the problems of those less fortunate in social standing, wealth, and education than he was. That was the conclusion of Frances Perkins, who had known him in the New York legislature and who believed he underwent a "spiritual transformation." His slightly arrogant attitude was gone, she said. "The man emerged completely warm-hearted with humility of spirit and with a deeper philosophy. Having been to the depths of trouble, he understood the problems of people in trouble." [8]

Possibly some of that was true, said his son James. But at heart, James claimed, his father had always cared about others. "I do not think, as has been suggested, that the ordeal of being crippled built father's character. I believe he had the basic strength of character to overcome his handicap." [9]

In spite of his illness, Roosevelt kept his job with Fidelity and Deposit, although much of his work was done by Louis Howe and Marguerite "Missy" LeHand, the personal secretary who was hired when he first went to the firm. He was still on the boards of many organizations: the Cathedral of St. John the Divine, New York's Boy Scout Foundation, and the Woodrow Wilson Foundation.

Once the plaster casts came off Roosevelt's legs in the spring of 1922, he put on his first set of steel braces, an admission by his doctors that his legs might never again support his weight. However, even then there was still some hope. If his case had really been a mild one, as his doctors had first said, he might still reactivate nerve cells in his spinal column and regain use of some leg muscles. But once two years had passed after his illness, it was unlikely his condition would change in any major way.

Kathleen Lake, a physiotherapist who visited him regularly to exercise his legs, taught him how to walk using the 14-pound clumsy and painful braces that ran from his feet to his waist and were strapped on with a leather band at the waist. He teetered along awkwardly and slowly, using a sort of rocking motion. With the crutches set in place slightly in front of his body, he threw his head forward and dragged his feet toward the crutches. Then he would throw his head back and move the crutches forward again. He hated the braces, said his son James. "Technicians learned to make lighter braces as time went on, but they never were comfortable and he always took them off whenever he could.''[10]

Meanwhile, the Roosevelt household smoldered with tension. Eleanor Roosevelt battled her rebellious teenage daughter, Anna, and clashed regularly with her mother-in-law. One afternoon, while reading to her sons, Eleanor started crying and could not stop. "The two little boys went off to bed and I sat on the sofa in the sitting room and sobbed and sobbed,'' she later wrote.[11]

So in May, Roosevelt and his nurse traveled to Hyde Park on his doctor's advice. At the Springwood estate, they believed, the atmosphere would be calmer and more soothing. He could get outside more often to practice walking with crutches. Eleanor and the children came to Hyde Park later, after school was out.

Thrilled at having her son home again, Sara had ramps built in the hallways of the house to handle his wheelchair. An old elevator that Franklin's father had once used to carry him between floors now took Franklin in his wheelchair upstairs.

Roosevelt quickly fell into the relaxing Hyde Park routine—sleeping late in the morning, exercising with his therapist, working on his model boats or stamp collections. Every year for the next few years, he spent several months this way at Hyde Park as he struggled to rebuild his legs.

But if Sara thought her son would pursue this lifestyle for the rest of his days, she was mistaken. "It was Louis Howe, more than anyone else, who forced father to fight back," said James Roosevelt. "And mother, through the urging of Louis. And Missy LeHand, though she seldom is given enough credit in this regard.''[12]

Not long after Roosevelt had become ill, Eleanor had asked Louis Howe if he really believed that Franklin still had a political future. "I believe,'' he answered, "that someday Franklin will be president.''[13]

7

"He is the 'Happy Warrior' "

While Roosevelt struggled to come back from his illness, he and his wife grew further apart. Early in his illness, her care for him had deepened his trust and respect for her, but Eleanor could never forget his romance with Lucy Mercer. They were more like friends and political partners than husband and wife.

Even before his bout with polio, she had been asserting her independence and seeking new friends and activities outside her family. Once the crisis in his disease had passed, she became more active outside the home again. She made two new friends, Marion Dickerman and Nancy Cook, who got Eleanor involved in the Women's Trade Union League and the women's division of the Democratic State Committee. Eleanor fought for better working conditions for laborers and a greater role for women in political parties. She became her husband's ambassador to the outside world and also a reporter who brought back news about politics to him.

She learned to do some things which before had

frightened her—like driving a car, even though it took her a number of fender-bender accidents to do so.

Louis Howe encouraged her interest in politics, believing that she could aid her husband in the future. But there were difficulties: she was plain and nervous and shy with a shrill speaking voice. Howe had her deliver dozens of speeches, with himself as her audience, until her confidence grew.

All the while Howe kept up contacts for his boss and persuaded Roosevelt to write to politicians on various issues. "I worked out a schedule for your father becoming president," he told James Roosevelt, "and we hit the timetable right on the button. He didn't know the details. . . . But I worked out in my mind when the right times to make our moves would be, and we made them." [1]

Roosevelt was focusing mainly on recovering the use of his legs. Through physical exercise he greatly developed his upper body so that he could use his hands, arms, and shoulders to lift and push himself to places he wanted to go.

His quest for physical fitness often led him on long trips away from his wife and family. With a friend, he bought a houseboat, the *Larooco,* and spent winter vacations on it in the Florida sunshine. Parties of friends went along and so did his devoted secretary, Missy LeHand, but Eleanor, who disliked the boating lifestyle, was seldom there. From the years 1925 to 1928, Roosevelt spent more than half of his time away from home and Missy LeHand was almost always with him.

LeHand came to work for Franklin as an attractive young woman in her twenties. After his illness she soon became more than a secretary: she encouraged him in his hobbies, she served as his hostess on the houseboat, she gave him political advice, she amused him and made him laugh as Eleanor could not, she was there when depression over his disability struck him.

Were they lovers as well as close friends and working

partners? Over the years, there has been much speculation over whether they had a romance. The true nature of their relationship has remained cloaked in mystery. "I suppose you could say they came to love one another," James Roosevelt said, "but it was not a physical love."[2]

Although Eleanor had refused to let Franklin continue his relationship with Lucy Mercer, for some reason she tolerated Missy LeHand although the situation aroused much gossip. Sara Roosevelt, for one, often objected that Eleanor did not spend more time with her husband.

Although Franklin Roosevelt still spent much of his time away from New York, he began to work at Fidelity and Deposit two or three mornings a week in the fall of 1922. But he did split from his law firm. Its type of legal business, mainly estates and wills, bored him. He formed a new partnership with a young man, Basil O'Connor, who seemed more aggressive and lively to Roosevelt than his old partners.

In the spring of 1923 Roosevelt traveled to Boston to see the polio expert, Dr. Lovett. The doctor was impressed with how well Roosevelt handled his crutches and braces, but his legs remained unchanged. Some of his muscles had actually grown weaker. The crucial two years since he had polio were almost up; the time for improvement was running out. But for several years, Roosevelt refused to accept the inevitable. He still pursued new exercises and treatments.

In the fall of 1924, Roosevelt's quest took him to Warm Springs, Georgia, where a Wall Street banker friend had part ownership in a ramshackle, aging resort hotel, the Meriwether Inn. The friend, George Foster Peabody, had told Roosevelt about a young polio patient who regained the use of his legs after bathing in the warm mineralized waters at Warm Springs.

At Warm Springs, Roosevelt met the young man, Lewis Joseph, who had gone from a wheelchair to using only canes. Together they worked out exercises for Roosevelt to try in the spring-fed pool where the water was naturally at 88 degrees. Roosevelt enjoyed the warm Georgia sunshine and found that in the buoyant water he could work for two hours at a time without getting tired or chilled. Eventually, he could walk unaided and unsupported across the pool, although outside its waters there was little change in his walking ability.

On the first trip, Eleanor had come along, but after a few days she was anxious to return to New York City and her new interests. She was disturbed that life in the South was "hard and poor and ugly" for so many people, white as well as black. "Even though I realized how greatly many people benefited from the place, I never really enjoyed living in Warm Springs as much as my husband did," she later wrote.[3]

Soon after Roosevelt arrived at Warm Springs, the Atlanta *Journal* sent a reporter to the resort to do a story on the former vice presidential candidate's activities. The paper then ran an upbeat Sunday magazine piece titled "Franklin D. Roosevelt Will Swim to Health" that described his belief that sunshine and swimming would help him overcome the effects of polio. The article was reprinted in other newspapers, and soon disabled polio patients from all over the country were writing to Roosevelt and Warm Springs. They wanted to come try the waters themselves.

Roosevelt and Tom Loyless, one of the co-owners of the hotel, were overwhelmed by the response and unsure of what to do. The resort was not well suited to taking on a flood of handicapped patients. There were no ramps and few bathrooms and no workers to help with therapy. But wheelchair ramps were installed, and cottages were spruced up. A new dining room was built for the polio patients that was separate from the one used by nondisabled guests. Roosevelt devised exercises and treatments. The patients who poured into Warm Springs called him "Dr. Roosevelt."

Finally, in 1926, Roosevelt decided to buy Warm Springs even though his family and friends and new law partner advised him not to. Eleanor was worried that the $200,000 he poured into the project, which represented two-thirds of his personal fortune, should be saved for their children's education, but Roosevelt assured her that his mother would always take care of the children if necessary.

He lobbied the American Orthopedic Association and got its endorsement of the hydrotherapeutic center at Warm Springs. He also hired a prominent New York doctor to run the Warm Springs treatment program. With his law partner he set up a special nonprofit foundation to run Warm Springs and to seek donations for its operation. Eventually, he turned the hotel and springs over to the foundation. Soon new buildings went up and new and more advanced equipment was installed. Patients found Warm Springs a warm and wonderful place compared to the strict, rigid hospitals where they had previously been treated.

Besides the hotel and its grounds, Roosevelt bought up large tracts of surrounding land for farming demonstrations to show the local poverty-stricken farmers how to make money off their land. But Roosevelt's experiments with pine trees, beef cattle, apples, peaches, and other crops never made a profit.

About that time, Roosevelt became more active politically. He had always had a game plan for his political life; polio had just set him back temporarily. As early as 1922 he had held a reception at his Hyde Park house in support of Al Smith, who was running for governor of New York.

Roosevelt had first met Smith back when they both served in the state legislature. They came from very different backgrounds. Roosevelt was the son of wealthy parents, raised in the country and educated at the best schools, and a world traveler as well; Smith was from a working-class New York City family and had grubbed and fought

73

his way to the top. He often called himself a graduate of the Fulton Fish Market. He had rarely been outside the urban areas of the East Coast. What made Smith even more unique in politics was that he was an Irish Catholic. For obvious reasons, Smith craved the support of the sophisticated, educated Roosevelt, who represented voters and classes with whom Smith had little contact.

Among other help that the Roosevelts gave to Smith, Eleanor went to the state Democratic Convention and led the Dutchess County delegation in a rally for Smith.

After Smith was elected, he proved to be a progressive-minded governor and a hero to working people. Under his leadership the legislature passed measures on rent control and public housing. He cleaned up the state administration and made it more efficient. Clearly, he was becoming a prime candidate for the Democratic nomination for the presidency in 1924.

At the same time, Louis Howe and Franklin Roosevelt both realized that it was very unlikely that a Democrat could win the presidency in 1924. Although the economy was shaky worldwide, somehow the Republicans managed to keep prosperity going in the United States.

On the other hand, the Republican incumbent President Warren Harding had allowed graft and corruption to run wild. Bribes were paid to Harding's secretary of the interior by oil company executives who wanted to pump out federally owned oil lands which were supposed to be kept reserved for a national emergency. This incident was called the Teapot Dome scandal, named after the dome of sandstone in Wyoming where the oil reserves lay.

Just as the scandal seemed ready to erupt into a political volcano for the Republicans, Warren Harding died on August 2, 1923, of a cerebral hemorrhage. His vice president, Calvin Coolidge, succeeded him. Coolidge was untainted by the scandals and moved to cancel the questionable oil leases and to punish the culprits.

But Smith pressed on with his quest for the White

House. In the spring of 1924 his staff asked Roosevelt to serve as the chairman of the Citizens' Committee for Smith. They were well aware of his disability, Smith's campaign staff told Roosevelt, but he need not do much work; they would do it all. Clearly, they wanted Roosevelt's endorsement because of his national reputation in politics and his social standing, but they did not want him too involved in the campaign.

Roosevelt, however, was not content to be a mere figurehead. He and Howe set up an office and issued hundreds of letters and press releases. Roosevelt tried to advise Smith about areas in which the candidate was inexperienced—farm relief and tariffs and foreign policy. Generally, Smith ignored Roosevelt and leaned on other politicians for his convention strategy.

But he did tap Roosevelt to give his nomination speech at the Democratic Convention held in the old Madison Square Garden in New York City. The speech had been written by another of Smith's advisers, Judge Joseph Proskauer. But Roosevelt strongly objected to the last few lines: "He has a power to strike at error and wrongdoing that makes his adversaries quail before him. He has a personality that carries to every hearer not only the sincerity but the righteousness of what he says. He is the 'Happy Warrior' of the political battlefield." [4]

The "Happy Warrior" section came from a poem by William Wordsworth, and Roosevelt thought it was too fancy for the kinds of Democrats who supported Al Smith. Roosevelt argued against the speech, but Proskauer insisted and finally Roosevelt agreed to deliver it. But he predicted that the speech would be a flop.

A difficult challenge lay ahead next for Roosevelt. How would he get to the speakers' platform to deliver the speech?

Each day of the convention, Roosevelt was brought by car to Madison Square Garden, where he was lifted into a wheelchair; he was then rolled inside by his teenage son

James. Once they were in the door, Roosevelt's braces were locked in position. Then, using James to support him by one arm and using a crutch in the other, he slowly inched to his oak armchair in the New York delegation. All this was done before a session so that as few delegates as possible could stare at him and so that Roosevelt could avoid the crowding in the aisles.

But on the day of the speech, he had to rise from that chair and walk up to the platform in full view of the convention audience. For days, he and James practiced walking the necessary distance, which they had measured off in the library of his New York City town house.

At noon on June 26, 1924, Roosevelt and James began their slow, painful walk up the convention hall aisle, while Eleanor and the other Roosevelt children watched from the gallery. Eleanor was so nervous that she had brought her knitting and could scarcely bear to watch.

"As we walked—struggled, really—down the aisle to the rear of the platform, he leaned heavily on my arm, gripping me so hard it hurt," James Roosevelt remembered. "It was hot, but the heat in that building did not alone account for the perspiration which beaded on his brow. His hands were wet. His breathing was labored. Leaning on me with one arm, working a crutch with the other, his legs locked stiffly in their braces, he went on his awkward way."[5]

Finally they stood at the rear of the speakers' platform. From there, Roosevelt wanted to walk alone up to the rostrum to deliver his speech. James handed him a second crutch, and Roosevelt moved slowly forward step by step across the 15 feet to the podium with almost the entire audience of 12,000 delegates holding its collective breath. He hitched his legs back and forth while shifting his crutches. His eyes focused steadily on the floor to keep track of where his feet were. James followed a few steps behind to catch him if he should fall.

Finally, he reached the lectern, and as he did, he threw

back his head and shoulders and triumphantly flashed his famous grin at the audience. The delegates stood and roared cheers and yells. When the standing ovation ended, his words rang out in a rich tenor. If he disliked the speech, no one in the audience knew it, because he made it very much his own. And when he gave the final "Happy Warrior" phrase at the end, the cheers rang out all over again and rocked the hall. To the thousands of delegates, Roosevelt was the "Happy Warrior"—not Smith. He was the one who had conquered adversity and overcome a crippling illness to return to the political battlefield again. Afterward, Roosevelt went home immediately to rest.

Despite the sparkle and emotion of Roosevelt's speech, it was not enough to carry Smith to victory. For thirteen days, the convention battled on and on over whom to nominate. The delegates were torn between Smith and William G. McAdoo, the son-in-law of Woodrow Wilson. In the end, after 103 ballots, they chose a compromise candidate, John W. Davis of West Virginia, a former ambassador to London.

To many, Roosevelt stood out as the real hero of the convention. The New York *Evening World* wrote about him: "Adversity has lifted him above the bickering, the religious bigotry, conflicting personal ambitions and petty sectional prejudices. It has made him the one leader commanding the respect and admiration of delegations from all sections of the land."[6]

8

"You've got to play the game"

After the 1924 convention, Roosevelt spent two years working on his legs—and much of that time was at Warm Springs. He wanted to return to the Democratic Convention in 1928 and walk to the platform without crutches. Although his progress was slow, by the 1926 New York State Democratic Convention he had learned to walk using a cane and crutch. After that, the physiotherapists at Warm Springs taught him how to walk using a single cane and another person as support. If he couldn't walk alone, he would learn to give the illusion that he was doing so.

Conveying the illusion of health and well-being had been a key part of Roosevelt's political plans from the first few weeks after polio struck him. He and Louis Howe tried to prevent the taking of photographs of him being carried from car to wheelchair or dock to boat or whatever. Often he was photographed while leaning against a wall or being supported by a friend—to give the impression that he was standing alone and unsupported. Only three photographs of him in his wheelchair have survived, although many photos show him looking athletic and vigorous while sitting on boats or swimming at Warm Springs. Newspaper photographers obligingly complied with Roosevelt's request that they not take embarrassing photos.

Because of the houseboat Roosevelt had bought, his children's private schools, and other expenses, money was very tight for him at this time. In 1925 he even had to sell some of his prized historical English and American naval and marine prints and paintings to raise money. As Eleanor had feared, Warm Springs proved a costly venture. Not only that, but he also agreed to Eleanor's request to build a small house and swimming pool in the woods about a mile and a half away from Springwood's main house. This cottage, known as Val Kill, was a retreat where she could stay with her newfound women friends, away from the intrusions of her dominating mother-in-law.

Franklin Roosevelt was never a particularly good businessman either. Over the years he had lost money in many schemes, including bonds, oil wells, shipping, and lobsters. His losses were never severe, but he remained dependent on his mother.

In spring 1928, however, Roosevelt's half brother, James, died at age seventy-three, leaving Franklin some money that eased his financial burdens.

In his 1924 bid for the presidential nomination, Al Smith had used Franklin Roosevelt as window dressing— someone who could bring him in contact with well-educated, wealthy Democrats but not someone whom he trusted very much or whom he could rely on for advice. But by 1928 that had changed. Smith, still governor of New York, was planning to seek the presidential nomination again, and this time he paid more attention to what Roosevelt had to say.

Smith had several problems to overcome. Although he had been a good governor, many Democrats were suspicious of him because he was a devout Roman Catholic. The Smiths had even visited the pope, and a cardinal had performed the wedding ceremony for their daughter. Anti-

Catholic feeling ran particularly high in the Southern states. Roosevelt pointed out to the Southern politicians that Smith had never allowed his religion to interfere with his job as governor, and he had Smith write a statement for the *Atlantic Monthly* magazine in which he said the Church could not have higher authority than the state.

Smith was also entangled in the national controversy over Prohibition, the ban on alcohol imposed by the Eighteenth Amendment to the Constitution. The "dry" Democrats of the South feuded constantly with the "wet" Democrats of the North over whether Prohibition should be repealed. Smith had favored modifying Prohibition to allow the sale of beer and wine. So he was labeled as a "wet." Roosevelt contended that regardless of his views, Smith would enforce the law and carry out the Eighteenth Amendment.

Roosevelt wanted Smith to make more trips out of New York State, to drum up more interest in his candidacy in other areas of the country. But for the most part, Smith stayed put.

The 1928 Democratic Convention met at the end of June in Houston, Texas. Although not all Democrats liked Smith, his opponents had failed to come up with an alternative candidate.

Roosevelt was floor manager for the Smith forces, and once again he made Smith's nominating speech. This speech was Roosevelt's chance to show the Democrats and the nation that he had recovered "fully" from his illness. He wanted the audience to view him as being lame but not crippled. He had shed his crutches and used only a cane.

Sam Houston Hall was boiling hot and jammed with 15,000 Democrats as Roosevelt moved across the auditorium and speakers' platform on the arm of his son Elliott. Roosevelt held a cane in his right hand and leaned his left arm on his son's right arm to take as much weight as possible off his body. He walked in a curious halting manner, using the muscles along the side of his trunk to hitch each leg forward. As they moved slowly along, he joked with Elliott, who had been instructed to smile broadly and look relaxed and happy. Roosevelt kept a grin on his face while the audience cheered wildly. Once at the lectern, he held on with one hand and waved with the other.

His audience was not only in the convention hall; another 15 million people were listening to him speak on the radio.

His speech was similar to the one he had given in 1924. He told the crowd about Smith: "Instinctively he senses the popular need because he himself has lived through the hardship, the labor and the sacrifice which must be endured by every man of heroic mold who struggles up to eminence from obscurity and low estate."[1] And once again he closed with the ringing words "The Happy Warrior, Alfred E. Smith."

Wild cheers and applause rose up from the crowd. And the press was wild in its praise as well. His speech, said the *New York Times,* "could not be heard or read without prompting to serious thought and sincere emotion."[2]

Will Durant, writing for the New York *World,* told his readers: "Here on the stage is Franklin Roosevelt, beyond comparison the finest man that has appeared at either convention. . . . A man softened and cleansed and illumined with pain."[3]

The convention went on to nominate Smith for the presidency on its very first ballot.

After the convention, Roosevelt planned to campaign hard for Al Smith. But following his triumphant speech at the convention, his fellow Democrats wanted much more from Roosevelt. However, he turned down the offers they made—the national chairmanship of the Democratic party and a chance to run for governor of New York.

His intent was to return to Warm Springs and work further to strengthen his legs. He still believed that in two or three years he could learn to walk alone. Anyway Louis

Howe and Roosevelt thought 1928 would be a bad year for the Democrats, even though they strongly supported Al Smith. For one thing, the Republicans had nominated a very strong presidential candidate, Herbert Hoover, who had won much acclaim during World War I.

Both Howe and Roosevelt believed that running for the governorship would be a poor move in 1928, even if Roosevelt won. If Hoover won election, he would probably be reelected in 1932 for another four years. Far better for Roosevelt to run for governor in 1932 and then for president in 1936, they thought.

Early in the race, Smith became tied to John J. Raskob, a top executive of General Motors and one of the wealthiest men in the nation. Both men were Catholics, both had worked their way to the top from poor families, both disliked Prohibition. Smith had Raskob appointed as chairman of the national Democratic Committee. The move alienated many liberal Democrats even though it brought in many contributions to the Smith campaign from big companies. In spite of his wealth Roosevelt had long criticized this means of campaign financing. He preferred to get small donations from millions of ordinary people to finance the campaign.

Smith and his advisers were not easily put off by Roosevelt's refusal to run for governor. That summer they visited Hyde Park to try to get Roosevelt to change his mind. It would help Smith win votes in upstate New York, they thought, if the popular Roosevelt was on the ticket. He hardly needed to campaign at all. But still Roosevelt, Howe, and Eleanor were opposed to Franklin's entering any kind of political race.

After Roosevelt went to Warm Springs in late September, Howe sent him a telegram: "My conviction that you should not run is stronger than ever and Eleanor agrees with me."[4] It was the first of many similar telegrams that Howe sent to Roosevelt to try to keep him from changing his mind. But Howe knew that as the Democrats prepared for the state convention on October 1, they still leaned toward having Roosevelt run for governor, despite his many refusals.

Al Smith's adviser Ed Flynn even phoned Roosevelt at Warm Springs. Again, Roosevelt said he could not run because of his many financial obligations at Warm Springs. But Flynn thought Roosevelt was wavering. Perhaps if the bills were paid for Warm Springs, Roosevelt might change his mind, he told Smith.

The days passed and the Democrats tried to come up with some other candidate for governor, but no one appealed to them as much as Roosevelt. The Republicans had nominated Albert Ottinger, the state attorney general famous for his crusades against stock fraud and food profiteers. So the Democrats wanted to field just as strong a candidate.

Smith and the Democratic leaders met and agreed Roosevelt just had to run. Roosevelt did not even have to do any work, they decided, because they could get a wealthy and competent New Yorker, Herbert Lehman, to serve as his lieutenant governor. Lehman could run New York State while Roosevelt concentrated on his health and exercises.

Of course, they still had to reach Roosevelt at Warm Springs and talk him into their plan. But it was difficult to reach him. No one at the Meriwether Hotel at Warm Springs seemed to know where he was. Telegram after telegram was sent to Georgia with no reply. Roosevelt saw the telegrams, of course, but decided that he would not call back.

Smith sought the help of Eleanor, who was visiting the state convention. He called her to his suite to ask her to persuade Roosevelt to run. "It is entirely up to him," she said. "I am not trying to influence him either way."[5]

Well, Smith said, would she at least call him on the phone so that Smith could talk to him? Eleanor agreed to do so, but getting through was still complicated.

A messenger finally contacted Roosevelt as he was about to make a speech at a high school in Manchester,

Georgia. His wife was on the phone at a drugstore down the street, he was told. After the speech, Roosevelt went to the drugstore to talk to Smith. But by then the connection had gone bad, and Roosevelt had to travel back to Warm Springs to take the call.

Riding to Warm Springs with Missy LeHand, he pondered the situation. Most of the members of his family opposed his running for governor. Louis Howe was still adamantly opposed. As they pulled into the hotel driveway, even Missy LeHand told him, "Don't you dare let them talk you into it."[6]

But on the phone he seemed to waver and Smith sensed this. "You take the nomination, Frank," he said. "You can make a couple of radio speeches and you'll be elected."[7] After that Roosevelt could return to Warm Springs and show up for only a month or so a year in Albany, Smith said. Then Lehman promised he would do everything he could if elected to ensure that Roosevelt could work almost full-time on his physical recovery. Smith's wealthy friend Raskob also offered to make large contributions to Warm Springs.

Finally Smith asked him: "If those fellows nominate you tomorrow and adjourn, will you refuse to run?"[8] Roosevelt hesitated; he didn't know what he would do, he told Smith, even though he wasn't sure he wanted to go back into public life.

That was enough for Smith, who told Roosevelt he wasn't about to ask any more questions. It was enough of a yes for the rest of the New York Democrats. The next day, Roosevelt's name was entered at the convention, and by acclamation he was chosen as the Democratic nominee. He was back in politics again full-time. It might be a bad election year for Democrats, but he was going to give all the strength he had to the campaign.

His family was upset. Eleanor sent him a telegram saying she regretted that he felt he had to run. Sara Roosevelt wrote to her son that she was also sorry about his entering the race "and yet if you run I do not want you to be defeated."[9] Louis Howe was still angry and unconvinced. He wired Roosevelt: "Mess is no name for it."[10]

But the next four weeks were full and happy ones for Roosevelt. As he told his chauffeur shortly after his final phone call from Al Smith: "When you're in politics, you've got to play the game."[11] And it was a game that Roosevelt loved.

He and Howe quickly mapped out their campaign strategy and set up an organization that included several men who would one day follow Roosevelt to the White House: James Farley, Henry Morgenthau, Jr., and Raymond Moley. A speech writer, Samuel Rosenman, was hired. Roosevelt's plan was to concentrate on upstate New York, where he had to win many Republican votes.

Very quickly, Roosevelt's health became an issue in the campaign. The Republican *New York Post* told its readers that Al Smith had been cruel to "draft" Roosevelt. "Even his own friends, out of love for him will hesitate to vote for him now," the paper's editorial writers said. Roosevelt should be allowed to go home and work on overcoming his paralysis.[12] Rumors spread that as soon as he was elected Roosevelt would resign and let Herbert Lehman, the lieutenant governor, take over the job.

Roosevelt responded strongly in a statement to the press which denied that he had been "dragooned" into running by Smith. He was drafted, he said, because Democratic leaders thought that he was the best man to continue the policies set by Al Smith as governor of New York. If he had a plea for his friends, Roosevelt said, he would tell them, "Not only do I want my friends to vote for me, but if they are my real friends I ask them to get as many other people to vote for me as possible."[13]

Soon Roosevelt was barnstorming in an open car in the towns and cities of upstate New York—Troy, Gloversville, Wellsville, Olean, Salamanca, Bath, Corning, Utica, Buffalo, Rochester. From October 17 until the end of the campaign, he traveled 1,300 miles and delivered dozens of speeches. Once he had to be carried up a fire escape and through a window to get to an auditorium. At times, he had to drag himself up and down stairways and ramps to reach inconvenient meeting halls.

But his strong smile and flashing eyes, his vigorous handshake and laughter impressed the crowds that had come out to see what this supposedly handicapped and severely ill man was like. Arriving in a town for an outdoor rally, he used a steel bar mounted at the back of the car's front seat to pull himself to a standing position. Then, with braces locked into place, he delivered a strong and impassioned speech for himself and on behalf of Alfred E. Smith, the presidential candidate. After telling one crowd about his hectic and energetic schedule, he joked, "Too bad about this unfortunate sick man, isn't it?" [14] And the audience cheered and laughed.

In his speeches he proposed adopting a new pension law for the elderly so that the poor among them would no longer have to go to the state's poorhouses. He urged better care for the disabled. When he became sick, he said, he had gotten the best care, but few New Yorkers could afford that. He proposed stronger control over the state's waterpower plants. The state should regulate its waterpower, he said, and protect the people's resources.

Finally, on November 6, Roosevelt was back in Hyde Park to vote at Town Hall. Then he traveled to a New York City hotel, where he and Eleanor waited with friends for the election results. As the votes rolled in, the situation seemed gloomy for Al Smith and for Roosevelt as well. The South, which had been expected to stick with Smith, was swinging over to Hoover. Evidently, Smith's religion and his opposition to Prohibition were having their effect. Not only that, but Smith was losing his home state, New York, as well.

Early returns indicated that Roosevelt was also losing even though he had won a big vote in New York City.

Howe was crushed, but Roosevelt's spirits remained good. One peculiar thing was happening—the results from upstate New York were only trickling in. Roosevelt's staff suspected that the Republicans were holding back returns until they could see how many votes they had to stuff in the ballot box to overcome Roosevelt's New York City total. So Roosevelt phoned the sheriffs in the slow counties and demanded that they make sure the voting was fair.

But still the totals seemed grim, and as hope died, Roosevelt and many of his supporters decided to go to bed. Among the few who lingered on through the night were Frances Perkins, the young woman lobbyist who had worked with Roosevelt in the state legislature, and Sara Roosevelt, keeping vigil for her son.

At about 2 A.M. their night of waiting was rewarded as new, surprising returns came in. "Forty votes here, one hundred votes there and seventy-five votes somewhere else," Perkins said. "They mounted up." [15]

When the final vote was in, Roosevelt had squeaked by Ottinger with 2,130,193 votes to 2,104,629 for his opponent. Because of the narrow margin of victory, it was more than a week before Ottinger conceded that he had lost and sent Roosevelt a letter of congratulations.

Roosevelt's recovery was complete. He had not regained the use of his legs, but he had regained his place in politics. His triumph awed a nation—a man victorious over one of the most dreaded diseases of all time.

9

"People aren't cattle!"

As Roosevelt headed for the governor's mansion in Albany, it was clear that the defeated presidential candidate, Al Smith, wanted a strong say in how Roosevelt ran the state of New York.

Smith believed that the state government under Roosevelt would actually be run by his former aide Belle Moskowitz; Herbert Lehman, the new lieutenant governor chosen by Smith; and Robert Moses, Smith's secretary of state. But Roosevelt had his own people in mind—like his neighbor Henry Morgenthau, Jr., who advised him on agricultural problems, Frances Perkins, who became head of the Department of Labor, and Sam Rosenman, the speech writer, who became counsel to the governor.

In a meeting before the inauguration, Smith pressed Roosevelt to hire Moskowitz and Moses. Roosevelt tried to be polite, but tension grew between the two men. Smith told Roosevelt that Mrs. Moskowitz was even writing an inaugural address for the new governor. "His first bad shock came when I told him that I had already prepared my inaugural address and that my message to the legislature was nearly finished,'' Roosevelt said. [1]

Although the two did not clash openly, Smith knew that the man he had thought was an invalid had a strong thirst for power. Roosevelt respected what Smith had done for the state, including building new parks and hospitals, setting limits on the work week for women, and reorganizing the hodgepodge of state agencies. But Roosevelt had his own plans.

On January 1, 1929, Roosevelt was sworn in and allowed Al Smith to give a farewell address. Afterward, Roosevelt and Smith stood on a reviewing stand amid a snowfall as an inaugural parade rolled by. Then a melancholy Smith left for the railroad station, leaving Roosevelt in charge.

From the very first, the executive mansion, a ramshackle Victorian house, was crammed with family and guests. When they were home from boarding school, the Roosevelt boys ran gleefully through the halls. Visitors crowded the nine guest bedrooms. Someone new was always coming to tea and dinner and lunch. There were many evening parties where Roosevelt and Eleanor charmed the flocks of guests.

At first, Eleanor Roosevelt had felt threatened by her husband's election. She had created a life for herself with her new friends that included supervising a furniture factory, built at her cottage at Val Kill, and teaching a couple of days a week at the Todhunter School in New York City, a private girls' school run by her friend Marion Dickerman. Moving to Albany to serve as first lady of New York could have ended all that, and she resisted. She continued to travel to New York City to teach and spent only a few days each week in Albany.

Roosevelt was only shortly into his term as governor when a financial crisis gripped the nation, one that would have important consequences for his career. During the summer of 1929 the overheated economy of the roaring

1920s had begun to cool down. Farmers struggled to make a living, construction of new buildings slowed down, sales of automobiles grew sluggish, unemployment rose. About the only part of the economy that remained strong was the stock market, and prices of many stocks rose to new and dizzying heights. By early September, General Electric stock was selling at 396 ¼, RCA at 505, and Westinghouse at 313. Many of these stocks had doubled and tripled their value since March. Although some financial forecasters warned that a crash was coming, few investors paid any attention.

But by late September, the stock market began to fall. Sharp declines followed until on October 24, 1929, hysteria swept the New York Stock Exchange. Worried buyers dumped their stocks in hopes of recovering a fraction of their investments. Finally, on October 29, 1929, more than 16 million shares were sold at huge losses, averaging about 25 points per issue. The Dow-Jones industrial average dropped 48 points. Although decades later the market dropped much more on a single day, the loss in 1929 was a financial catastrophe never seen before. The paper losses on that day were several times the total amount of money in circulation in the United States.

Eventually, Americans realized that the stock market crash had signaled the start of what was called the Great Depression. But at first almost no one in government or business realized that the boom of the 1920s had fizzled and died. President Herbert Hoover was actually among those who realized that the economy had suffered a serious blow.

Although Hoover was a Republican, generally committed to the idea that business works best if left alone, he organized meetings in early November to get factory owners, financiers, and builders to promise that they would not lay off workers or slash wages. He speeded up public building projects so that more workers could get jobs constructing parks, roads, and bridges. He pushed through

Congress a new tariff to raise prices on foreign goods so that American businesses would have an advantage in selling their products.

But the economy spiraled downward, and instead of acting more firmly, Hoover did less. He decided that his efforts to boost employment might be making business leaders gloomy and pessimistic. Far better to build up the public's confidence, he decided, and tell America it would soon be prosperous again. "We have now passed the worst," he said, "and with continued unity of effort we shall rapidly recover."[2]

But by the spring of 1930, 4 million Americans were unemployed, and by the spring of 1931 that number had jumped to 8 million. Those who still had their jobs were often working only two or three days a week. The families of the unemployed struggled to make do with less and less and used up their savings. Millions of Americans went on relief—welfare payments that cities and counties and local charities tried to provide. But these agencies had little in reserve for such massive suffering, and many families received as little as $2 a week in aid. The idea that the state or federal government might step in and provide more aid was difficult for Hoover and many politicians to accept. It seemed to undermine a basic tenet of democracy: that men and women could succeed through hard work and individual effort.

In the summer of 1930 a massive drought swept through the Southwest, killing cattle and crops. Hoover got Congress to put up government loans to help farmers buy seed, fertilizer, and cattle feed. A number of Democratic senators suggested that Hoover go farther and distribute surplus wheat purchased by federal farm agencies to the poor and unemployed. Hoover refused. Federal aid, he said, would destroy the backbone of individualism that held the nation together.

Early in the Depression, Franklin Roosevelt too seemed slow to recognize how serious the financial crisis was. But by early 1930 he had decided that the unemployment situation in New York was growing serious. He pushed plans to enforce child labor laws more strictly so that children wouldn't take jobs away from adults, to increase old-age pensions so that older people could retire and make way for the unemployed, and to adopt a five-day work week by law.

Often while Roosevelt served as governor, Republicans tried to draw strong links between him and the popular but incompetent mayor of New York, Jimmy Walker, whose organization had become very corrupt. Republicans demanded that Roosevelt clean up the mess in New York City, but he was hesitant. Walker was a product of Tammany Hall, and Roosevelt had long since made his peace with Tammany, which loyally supported him.

Finally, news broke that some city judges had paid bribes to Tammany Hall to get their jobs, and Roosevelt had to act or he would look as if he condoned corruption. He ordered an investigation headed by the state's attorney general and also asked some prominent court officials to conduct an inquiry. He ordered Walker and his assistants to cooperate in the investigation. But it wasn't until the very end of Roosevelt's years as governor of New York that Walker was forced to resign.

Although Roosevelt had wavered in the Walker matter, it did not seem to hurt his popularity with voters, who seemed to accept corruption in New York City as a fact of life.

Roosevelt also managed to avoid political damage in the growing national fight over Prohibition, the federal ban on the manufacture and sale of alcoholic liquor. Although Prohibition had been the law for a number of years, liquor was still produced illegally by violent professional gangs, and police seemed unable or unwilling to enforce the ban. As a result, many Americans favored the repeal of Prohibition, but others seemed strongly opposed. Roosevelt tried to satisfy both the "wets" and the "drys." The question of alcohol should be left up to the states, he said. Those states that still wanted to ban alcohol could do so, he said.

Even before he was elected governor of New York, many Democrats had viewed Roosevelt as a candidate who could win the White House in 1932. But before he could push on to that goal, he faced a reelection race in 1930 for another two-year term as governor. The odds seemed strongly in his favor, but he had to roll up a massive win to prove that he could be a national candidate.

Roosevelt's Republican opponent was Charles H. Tuttle, the U.S. attorney for New York City and the very man who had been digging away at all the corruption in Tammany Hall and New York mayor Jimmy Walker's administration. Tuttle continued to expose judges who had taken bribes, and Roosevelt procrastinated about cleaning up the mess. But Tuttle also proved a weak campaigner. The corruption scandals had become so complicated that few voters could keep track of who the culprits were and what they had done. Many upstate voters, especially Republicans, felt that Tuttle had failed to develop any positive proposals for the governor's office involving waterpower and farm problems. All he seemed able to do was hammer away at the evils of New York City politics.

During the race, Roosevelt made points with voters by his attacks on President Hoover and the Republicans over how they handled the stock market crash and Depression. The Republicans should have taken steps in 1928 to prevent the market from overheating, Roosevelt said. They could have avoided the disaster on Wall Street.

Hoover sensed that the nation was watching the New York race very closely, and he sent his secretary of state, Henry L. Stimson, and several other high-level officials to campaign for Tuttle. They hit Roosevelt hard over the corruption issue. Roosevelt responded by asking why these federal officials wanted to tell the people of New York how to solve their problems.

The election was a rousing landslide for Roosevelt.

Not only did he take New York City, where he had expected an easy victory, but he also won the upstate vote as well. He had a statewide plurality of more than 725,000 votes. In beating Charles Tuttle he had shown Hoover and the Republicans that he was a serious threat for 1932. The day after the election, humorist Will Rogers commented, "The Democrats nominated their President yesterday, Franklin D. Roosevelt."[3]

As Roosevelt dealt more and more with the Great Depression during this second term, he indeed looked like presidential material to a nation hungry for new ideas and a fresh approach to its economic problems. Like many politicians of his day, Roosevelt had begun by believing that unemployment and the need for relief money to help the poor and jobless had to be handled locally; he at first rejected the idea that the state and federal governments should get involved. But gradually Roosevelt changed his mind; he was always open to new ideas and proposals.

Shortly after his reelection, he held a governors' conference in Albany with a young liberal economist from the University of Chicago, Paul H. Douglas. The group discussed the idea of unemployment insurance, payments that would be made to workers by the government when they lost their jobs.

Although no immediate proposals came out of the conference, the discussions helped persuade Roosevelt that the whole nation needed unemployment insurance and that the federal or state government must set up the system. He eventually came out publicly for this insurance in a major speech to a nationwide conference of governors.

He believed that government must get involved in the crisis. It was not enough to let the economy plunge to the bottom and then rise again naturally. Too many people could get hurt in the process. On one occasion Frances Perkins listened to an economist argue this point with Roosevelt. "I shall never forget the gray look of horror on his face," Perkins said, "as he turned on this man and said, 'People aren't cattle, you know!' "[4]

In one important area, Roosevelt clung to old ideas and allegiances. Perhaps because he had once worked on Wall Street himself and because he had so many old school friends in the banking and financial industry, he believed that bankers knew what they were doing.

Early in Roosevelt's first term as governor, he was warned that banks in New York City were on the verge of collapse. The safety of the deposits of millions of New Yorkers was threatened. The warning had come in a report done by Robert Moses, an adviser to former governor Al Smith. But Roosevelt had ignored the report's recommendations that he crack down on the bankers, partly because Moses was an old political enemy.

Roosevelt's inaction led to a disaster. In the fall of 1930, rumors swept New York that the Bank of the United States, which held some 450,000 deposits, was in trouble. Frightened people lined up for hours in the rain outside the bank to try to retrieve their money. Just before Christmas the state was forced to close the bank, jeopardizing the savings of thousands of small depositors. Soon other banks shut down. Only then did Roosevelt go to the legislature to ask for new laws that would provide more safeguards for depositors.

In another matter in dealing with the Depression, Roosevelt was a pioneer. As the winter of 1931 approached, all across the country the situation for the poor and unemployed was growing more desperate. No longer could cities and towns and private charities handle the problem, he decided. In one of his speeches he declared, "Modern society acting through its government, owes the definite obligation to prevent the starvation or the dire want of any of its fellow men and women who try to maintain themselves but cannot."[5]

In a special session of the legislature, Roosevelt asked

for new relief payments for the poor, which were to be supported by higher taxes. Like President Hoover, Roosevelt then believed that any relief given must be temporary—not a permanent "dole" for the poor. The Temporary Emergency Relief Administration set up in New York was the first state agency of its kind and was copied by other states. Headed by Harry L. Hopkins, a young man who later became Roosevelt's right-hand man in the White House, the administration was soon giving about 10 percent of the families in the state an average of $23 a month. Roosevelt was not as far ahead in his thinking as some other liberals, who wanted more-extensive aid for the poor, but he was first among state governors to act. Throughout the nation he was regarded as a champion of the little guy, a man who dared to help the down-and-out in new and different ways.

*Above: FDR as a child
at Hyde Park, seated on
a donkey with dog Budgy
Left: Roosevelt, with father
James Roosevelt and mother
Sara, in 1899*

As manager of the Groton School baseball team, back row, third from right

As president of The Harvard Crimson, *Roosevelt (front row, center) posed with other members of the newspaper's senior board.*

Eleanor and Franklin at the time of their engagement. "In the autumn of 1903, when Franklin Roosevelt, my fifth cousin once-removed, asked me to marry him it seemed an entirely natural thing and though I was only nineteen, I never even thought that we were both rather young and inexperienced," Eleanor later wrote.

*Above: As assistant secretary
of the Navy, Roosevelt,
second from left, returns
home from Europe with
President and Mrs. Wilson
(backs to camera)
in February 1919.*

*Left: At Hyde Park,
Roosevelt accepts the
nomination as vice
presidential running mate
of Governor James M. Cox
of Ohio, summer, 1920.*

*View of the Roosevelt home at
Hyde Park, New York*

*Franklin and Eleanor, with Sara Roosevelt between them,
pose for a photo with their children (left to right)
Elliott, Franklin, Jr., John, Anna, and James.*

*Campobello House, in the Bay of Fundy in New Brunswick,
Canada, where Roosevelt was first stricken with polio*

Left: At Hyde Park with John W. Davis, 1924 Democratic nominee for president, not long after Roosevelt's "Happy Warrior" speech in support of the candidacy of New York Governor Al Smith

Below: Roosevelt takes oath of office for governor of New York, January 1, 1931, with Eleanor standing behind.

*Left: Scene of the
Great Depression – a bread
line in New York City,
Christmas Day, 1931.
The way was clear
for Roosevelt's ascent
to the White House.*

*Below: Roosevelt, arriving
in Chicago to accept the
Democratic nomination for
president, July 2, 1932*

Left: FDR, making his first presidential nomination acceptance speech

Below: National Recovery Administration (NRA) float on parade in 1933. The NRA allowed businesses to enter into agreements to stabilize prices and production. It also advocated fair wages and hours for workers.

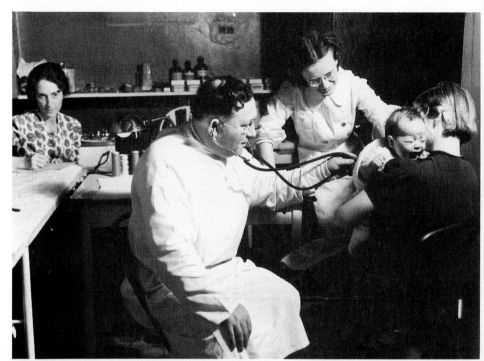

Examples of two New Deal programs: Top, Works Progress Administration (WPA) nurse assists doctor at a clinic in Louisville, Kentucky. Bottom, production of Shakespeare's Macbeth *put on by the Negro Theatre Unit of the WPA's Federal Theatre Project.*

*WPA funds were used to build
this school in Old Lyme, Connecticut,
top, which replaced five one-room
schools like the one below.*

Above: In 1940, many people
had reservations about
electing Roosevelt to an
unprecedented third term
as president. Roosevelt
had a vigorous challenger
in Republican nominee
Wendell Willkie, but
nevertheless easily prevailed.

Left: Roosevelt, meeting with
British Prime Minister
Winston Churchill aboard a
ship in the Atlantic Ocean
on August 14, 1941.
They issued a proclamation
known as the "Atlantic Charter,"
in which they called
for a world free of
fear and want.

Above: smoking hulk of the USS Arizona, *after it was bombed and sunk by the Japanese at Pearl Harbor, Hawaii, on the morning of December 7, 1941*

Left: Roosevelt making his "day of infamy" speech to Congress, in which he asked for a declaration of war against Japan

*The Allied "Big Three"—Stalin, Roosevelt, and Churchill—
meet in Tehran, Iran, in late 1943. It is interesting to note that,
of the three, only Roosevelt was dressed in civilian clothes (Churchill
wears the uniform of a Royal Air Force marshal).*

*Roosevelt receiving a briefing on Pacific war strategy from Admiral
Chester W. Nimitz. To his right is General Douglas MacArthur.*

*U.S. soldiers fire a flamethrower
against a Japanese bunker on
Kwajalein Island in the Pacific in 1944.*

*Eleanor and family stand at graveside during burial services
for FDR at Hyde Park, April 16, 1945.*

American flag is lowered to half-mast at American army outpost in Germany after the death of the commander-in-chief.

10

"To the next president of the United States!"

For years, Franklin Roosevelt had been viewed as a possible presidential candidate. When he became governor in Albany, his old friend and adviser, Louis Howe, stayed in New York City to run what amounted to Roosevelt's presidential campaign office, although neither Roosevelt nor Howe said that openly. It was not good to look too eager to be president. In 1929, shortly after being elected governor, Roosevelt wrote to a newspaper editor: "I am definitely disturbed by purely speculative and wholly false . . . statements about any considerations which I am giving to national candidacy." [1]

But still Roosevelt appealed to the public. What the average voter especially liked was his increasing insistence that the government find new ways to deal with the Depression. The government, he said, had to deal with "the forgotten man" at the bottom of the economy, not the businessmen and banks at the top. [2]

Except for the Socialist and Communist party candidates, Roosevelt was the only candidate, according to historian Arthur Schlesinger, Jr., to criticize big business and to demand that government experiment with changing the economic system. He was vague about what these new ideas might be; he had not come up with concrete proposals himself. But to the man and woman on the street he looked like the champion who could save them from joblessness and starvation.

Shortly after Roosevelt's reelection as governor, he began to campaign in earnest for the presidency, although he still had not announced his intentions openly. Fundraising began, and one of his trusted advisers, James Farley, traveled the country to renew old friendships for Roosevelt and organize local workers. In one nineteen-day trip in 1931, Farley met with 1,100 local Democratic leaders.

But while workers at the bottom were excited about Roosevelt entering the race, the leaders of the Democratic party grew angry. Strongly opposed to Roosevelt was John J. Raskob, Al Smith's millionaire friend and the chairman of the Democratic party. Raskob wanted Smith to run again even though Smith kept telling all his friends he did not want to be a candidate.

But as it became clear that whoever ran for president as a Democrat in 1932 would certainly be elected, Smith changed his mind. He wanted to vindicate himself against all the bigots who had voted against him just because he was Catholic. His old anger at Roosevelt grew. In the fall of 1931 Roosevelt put on the ballot for a public vote a reforestation bond issue to pay for planting seedlings on barren land, one of Roosevelt's pet projects. Lumber groups, conservationists, sportsmen, and farmers supported the idea, but Smith opposed it in several speeches. On election day the measure was overwhelmingly approved. In the first test of Roosevelt versus Smith, Roosevelt had won.

Shortly after that, one of Roosevelt's strongest supporters, Clark Howell, the publisher of the Atlanta *Constitution*, visited Smith to seek his support for Roosevelt in the presidential election, but Smith refused. Why did Smith dislike Roosevelt so much? Howell asked.

Roosevelt had always been kind to him, Smith said.

Socially, he considered Roosevelt a friend. But he added angrily: "Do you know, by God, that he has never consulted me about a damn thing since he has been governor? He has taken bad advice and from sources not friendly to me. He has ignored me!"[3]

Early in the presidential nomination campaign, Roosevelt faced new questions about his health. Everywhere Farley traveled, he had to assure local Democrats that Roosevelt was strong enough to be president in spite of his disabled legs. "I find that there is a deliberate attempt to create the impression that my health is such as would make it impossible for me to fulfill the duties of president," Roosevelt wrote to a friend.[4]

To head off these whispers and rumors, a reporter friend of Roosevelt's arranged for him to be examined by a committee of expert doctors. They declared that Roosevelt was thoroughly fit to serve in public office. The reporter then wrote up the findings in *Liberty* magazine, putting to rest most of the questions about Franklin Roosevelt's health.

In January 1932 Roosevelt formally announced his candidacy. It was early in the campaign, but almost immediately Roosevelt began picking up delegates pledged to vote for him at the Democratic Convention—six from Alaska, sixteen from Washington State, nine from North Dakota. Although Smith declared that he would run shortly after Roosevelt made his announcement, he and the other contenders for the nomination were far behind Roosevelt with his tightly run organization.

Several congressmen who felt that Roosevelt was a sure winner began to swing new delegates to his side, but Raskob and Jouett Shouse, whom Raskob hired as full-time director of the Democratic party, had a plan to stop Roosevelt. They wanted to recruit as many favorite-son candidates to run as possible. That way they could split up the vote enough to prevent Roosevelt from winning a needed two-thirds majority on the first ballot.

Among these candidates were Governor Albert Ritchie of Maryland, Governor W. H. Murray of Oklahoma, and Newton Baker, the progressive mayor of Cleveland. Perhaps the strongest rival was John Nance Garner of Texas, Speaker of the House of Representatives, who appealed to Democrats in the West because he favored taking strong action in the Depression and supported Prohibition.

Despite growing support for Roosevelt, many intellectuals, including major newspaper columnists, were upset with him. He had steered a middle course on several key issues, including whether Prohibition should be abolished and whether the United States should enter the League of Nations. He was not progressive enough for them. They were also displeased that he failed to crack down strongly on the corruption in Tammany Hall. "Franklin Roosevelt is no crusader," said Walter Lippmann, columnist for the New York *Herald Tribune*. "He is no tribune of the people. He is no enemy of entrenched privilege. He is a pleasant man who, without any important qualifications for the office, would very much like to be president."[5]

Liberals grew even more disturbed when Roosevelt finally announced that he no longer favored entering the League of Nations. He took this stand, he said, because "the League of Nations today is not the league conceived by Woodrow Wilson."[6] Roosevelt made this statement to win the support of newspaper magnate William Randolph Hearst. To many liberals and progressives it seemed that Roosevelt, a former apostle of Woodrow Wilson, was betraying much that Wilson stood for.

In April 1932 Smith launched a fierce attack on Roosevelt at the Democrats' annual Jefferson Day dinner. All the major candidates for governor were invited to sit on the speakers' platform—all but Franklin Roosevelt. At the dinner Smith attacked Roosevelt, although he didn't actually mention his name. Roosevelt's appeals to the people, Smith implied, were the actions of a demagogue—one who champions popular causes and makes false promises purely to win power. "I protest against the endeavor to delude the poor people of this country to their ruin by trying to make them believe that they can get employment before the people who would ordinarily employ them are also again restored to conditions of normal prosperity,'' Smith said.[7]

In spite of this opposition, Roosevelt swept strongly through the primaries. Georgia, Iowa, Maine, Wisconsin, Nebraska, Michigan, and Kentucky—he won them all. But in late April, Smith won the Massachusetts primary, and in May, Garner won California, with Roosevelt scoring a weak second.

Some editorial writers predicted that Roosevelt was finished, but soon he scooped up delegate votes in more primaries across the country. Clearly, he would go to the convention with a majority of the possible votes. But could he win the two-thirds vote necessary? Or would the convention be deadlocked, allowing a dark horse to steal the prize?

In June the Republicans met in Chicago and renominated Herbert Hoover, but with little enthusiasm. They knew that unless the economy had a strong upswing, Hoover was likely to lose in November.

Later that month the Democrats also went to Chicago for their convention. Al Smith and the other Democratic front-runners were there and were soon nicknamed the ''Allies'' because of their joint efforts to stop Roosevelt. Smith denied that he was there simply to block Roosevelt's nomination, insisting that he wanted to be nominated himself.

Meanwhile, Franklin Roosevelt remained with his family in the governor's mansion in Albany, New York. But his chief aides, Louis Howe, Ed Flynn, and Jim Farley, were in Chicago and talked to him constantly via a direct phone line.

Roosevelt's first real test at the convention came when he and his advisers tried to get delegates to overturn the rule requiring nomination of a presidential candidate via a two-thirds vote. But even Roosevelt's Tammany Hall sup-

101

porters refused to give in and approve a majority vote. Roosevelt finally had to back down. It was an embarrassing situation; it looked as if his support had been slipping away.

On Thursday, nominations were entered for candidates. With the large crowd of contenders, the speeches and the demonstrations droned on and on for hours. Farley and Flynn moved to and fro among the delegates to bolster weak links and swing new votes to Roosevelt. They predicted to everyone that Roosevelt would win on the first ballot despite the two-thirds rule. Howe kept phoning Roosevelt on the situation.

Back in Albany, Roosevelt and his family hovered around the radio listening to the convention news and wondering what the outcome would be.

Balloting on the candidates finally began at four–twenty-eight in the morning. On the first ballot Roosevelt had 666¼ votes, 89 more than a majority and 464½ ahead of Smith, his closest rival. But he was still 104 votes short of the needed two-thirds majority. He had not gotten the first-ballot victory his aides had predicted.

The delegates moved on to a second ballot, with Roosevelt's staff working madly to pick up a few more votes for him so that it wouldn't look as if his support had been slipping. Farley pried 6 votes loose from the Missouri delegation. On the third ballot Farley managed to pull Roosevelt's total up to 682—still short of the two-thirds majority. But by then it was nine-fifteen in the morning and the exhausted delegates were ready to adjourn until the evening.

Full of confidence, Roosevelt's opponents returned to their hotel rooms. They had not stopped him yet, but they were sure his workers could not hold his votes together much longer.

All day long, Farley negotiated with the Texas delegation, which solidly backed Garner. The Texas delegates still wanted their man in the White House, but Garner was realistic. He believed that if the convention were dead-locked, the Democrats would end up picking a weak compromise candidate who could not beat President Hoover. He was ready to step aside to prevent that. He preferred to see Roosevelt get the nomination.

The only problem was that Texas would not swing to Roosevelt unless he offered Garner the vice presidency. Roosevelt did so, and Garner agreed to join the ticket even though he disliked giving up his powerful post as Speaker of the House for the less powerful job of vice president. Once Garner released the Texas delegation, the California delegation also swung from Garner to Roosevelt.

When the head of the California delegation announced the news, the Roosevelt delegates cheered and applauded, but there were hisses and boos from the galleries, which were still packed with Smith's supporters. Smith had remained in his hotel; he could not stand to watch Roosevelt's triumph.

At 10:32 that evening the voting was complete; the convention chairman proclaimed that Roosevelt, with 945 votes, was the Democratic nominee for president of the United States.

In the past, nominees had always waited several weeks to formally accept the nomination. But the times in America called for dynamic action, Roosevelt felt, so he flew to Chicago to give his acceptance speech. The idea of a candidate flying to the convention startled and thrilled delegates.

At 7:25 A.M. on July 2 he boarded a trimotor airplane at the Albany airport. Traveling with him were Eleanor, their sons Elliott and John, a contingent of secretaries and bodyguards, and Sam Rosenman, who was polishing up Roosevelt's acceptance speech.

Air travel was in its crude early days, and the plane bumped slowly toward Chicago through squalls and head winds. It had to land twice to refuel. Finally, at 4:39 P.M., Roosevelt landed in Chicago, where cheering crowds greeted his plane. By six, he was in the convention hall to give his speech. "I regret that I am late," he told the delegates, "but I have no control over the winds of Heaven." [8]

America needed a new outlook, he said. The Democratic party had to be a party of liberal thought and progressive action.

He talked about the Depression and its impact on America. He talked about his proposals: repeal of Prohibition, more controls for the stock market, a federal program of public works, a shorter workweek. He offered jobs and security to the people of the United States.

The words that especially stirred the nation and that set the tone for the next four years were his conclusion: "I pledge you, I pledge myself, to a new deal for the American people. Let us all here assembled constitute ourselves prophets of a new order of competence and of courage. This is more than a political campaign; it is a call to arms. Give me your help, not to win votes alone, but to win in this crusade to restore America to its own people." [9]

The phrase "new deal" caught the imagination of the press and of all who heard it. Cheers rocked the hall.

As Roosevelt's campaign began, some of his advisers had urged him to stay home and use radio broadcasts to get his message across. After all, the Republicans were in such deep trouble that he seemed to have the election locked up. But he wanted to conduct a grassroots campaign among the voters themselves. He particularly wanted to travel in the West, an area that was crucial for him to win.

Before the nomination he had assembled a "brain trust," a group of university professors to advise him on policy matters. Among them were Raymond Moley, Rexford Guy Tugwell, and Adolf A. Berle, Jr. Rosenman and Roosevelt's law partner, Basil O'Connor, ran the group, which served not just as Roosevelt's advisers but also as his teachers. As the weeks passed, new advisers were added to the brain trust. But Roosevelt remained in charge of setting policy.

Although he had talked about taking strong action in his nomination speech, the truth was that he was still deciding what his administration would be like. He felt he had to keep his mind open—to try new ideas whenever they came along. "If we can't get a president with a fluid mind," he told one adviser, "we shall have some bad times ahead." [10]

Both liberal and conservative Democrats pressured him to adopt policies they favored. His own running mate, John Garner, told one of Roosevelt's advisers that he thought Roosevelt might be too liberal: "We will all follow him to hell if we have to, but if he goes too far with some of these wild-eyed ideas we are going to have the s--t kicked out of us." [11]

Garner believed that the federal government had already gone too far in taking power away from the states in an effort to curb the Depression. Other conservative Democrats pushed for a balanced budget and cuts in federal spending, the same actions that the Republicans favored.

The liberal wing of the party urged that Roosevelt increase social programs that required major changes in the federal government. Some brain trusters, such as Harvard law professor Felix Frankfurter, proposed that Roosevelt concentrate on regulating banks and securities and breaking up large corporations. These conflicting ideas often sparked arguments among Roosevelt's advisers.

In September in San Francisco, Roosevelt gave a key speech to the Commonwealth Club to outline where he was headed. The age of expansion and growth was over, he told the audience. The United States had no frontier left, no free land. Most American people lived in cities, not on farms. More and more, large corporations were taking over businesses in the nation.

Government had to step in to regulate the economic system and to restrict speculators, manipulators, and financiers, he said. "Our task now is not discovery or exploitation of national resources and plants already in hand, it

105

is the soberer, less dramatic business of administering resources and plants already in hand, of seeking to reestablish foreign markets for our surplus production, of meeting the problem of underconsumption, of adjusting production to consumption, of distributing wealth and products more equitably, of adapting existing economic organizations to the service of the people. The day of the enlightened administration has come," he said.[12]

This remarkable speech set the tone for much of what Roosevelt did in the future. But at times Roosevelt could still be inconsistent about what he wanted. Hoover had been attacking his opponent, Roosevelt, as a freewheeling government spender. So Roosevelt gave a speech in October in Pittsburgh in which he attacked the Republicans for deficit spending and promised to reduce the cost of federal government operations by 25 percent. He pledged himself to reorganize and retrench in Washington. In later years Roosevelt would regret taking this stand, which conflicted with much of what he wanted to do.

Roosevelt also began the campaign proposing to cut the tariffs that raised the prices of foreign goods and products imported into the United States. But Hoover attacked him on this issue as well. So Roosevelt backtracked, promising to leave the tariffs alone on farm products. On the one hand the tariffs protected American farmers, but on the other hand they kept foreign producers from selling their goods in the United States and raising money to pay for what they wanted to buy from America.

During a railroad tour in the West, Roosevelt drew huge crowds at each train stop. He would go to the platform in the last car on the arm of his eldest son, James, often accompanied by other relatives. He would talk a few minutes, tell a joke or two, and wave good-bye. He seemed to have enormous physical strength. "Roosevelt smiles and smiles and smiles and it doesn't get tiresome," one reporter wrote.[13]

At first the great crowds were silent and solemn, dissatisfied with their president in Washington, but still unsure of whether Roosevelt was the man of the hour. But gradually they warmed to him and their enthusiasm and cheers grew stronger. "I have looked into the faces of thousands of Americans," Roosevelt said. "They have the frightened look of children . . . they are saying: 'We're caught in something we don't understand; perhaps this fellow can help us out.' "[14]

Meanwhile, Hoover got a chilly reception around the country. In Des Moines, farmers greeted him with banners reading, "In Hoover we trusted; now we are busted." At the Detroit train station he was roundly booed.

But he kept fighting and told the nation that the struggle between Roosevelt and him was a contest between two philosophies of government. Roosevelt, he said, was proposing changes and "so-called new deals which would destroy the very foundations of our American system."[15]

From the start of the campaign, polls had shown that Roosevelt led Hoover by a large margin. On Election Day, November 8, the Roosevelts went to the polls in Hyde Park and were swamped by photographers and newsreel camera people. That evening they went to New York City for a small dinner party for friends and advisers. Early in the evening two Secret Service men came to stand guard, in anticipation of what was to come.

After dinner Roosevelt went to the Biltmore Hotel to await the returns. Farley and Flynn were there. Howe remained in campaign headquarters; he had last-minute doubts that Roosevelt could win. But very early the returns showed that there would be a huge victory for Roosevelt, one that would ensure power for the Democrats in the White House for decades to come.

He carried forty-two states, and Hoover carried only six. He received a popular vote of 22.8 million, compared with 15.75 million for Hoover.

Finally, even Howe had to admit that Roosevelt had won. At eleven o'clock, when Eleanor Roosevelt came to the office to persuade him to join the campaign party, Howe took a bottle of sherry out of his desk. He had put it away twenty years before, promising not to open it until Roosevelt became president. He raised his glass in a toast: ''To the next president of the United States!'' [16]

11

"The only thing we have to fear is fear itself"

The winter of 1932–33 was filled with gloom and despair as the nation waited for Franklin Roosevelt to take the oath of office in the spring.

More than 15 million people had lost their jobs. The nation's banking system teetered near collapse with hundreds of banks closing down. Almost every industry—automobiles, coal, gasoline, building—had cut back production because their products no longer sold. Unemployed workers fled the cities for the farms, but in the country a wave of mortgage foreclosures took land away from small farmers. Children across the nation went hungry—in Chicago, teachers chipped in money from their salaries to pay for free lunches for half-starved students.

People who could not pay their power bills had to light their homes with candles. In New York City a homeless couple moved into a cave in Central Park, where they lived for a year. In Philadelphia one family reportedly lived eleven days on only stale bread bought at 3½ cents a loaf.

To many, even to those who had voted for Franklin Roosevelt, it seemed unlikely that he or anyone could lift the nation out of this despair. As he awaited the inauguration he seemed outwardly calm and genial, almost detached from the struggles ahead. He met his advisers and picked his Cabinet, but he gave little clue to business and congressional leaders about his plans for the future. Of course, he had hinted about what the New Deal might do in speeches made around the country before the election. He had talked about a reforestation program to employ youth, about government regulation of utilities and Wall Street, about the need to revamp the welfare system.

As the crisis deepened, Roosevelt faced strong pressure from the almost panic-stricken Herbert Hoover. Hoover wanted Roosevelt to promise publicly that he would not inflate the currency or plunge the government into deficit spending. Otherwise, said Hoover, the nation's banking system might collapse. Hoover insisted that the economy was improving and that Roosevelt must not make drastic changes. But Roosevelt refused to make any promises. To his advisers he betrayed no anxiety about the challenges ahead.

Before the inauguration Roosevelt visited Warm Springs and also took a twelve-day fishing cruise down the Florida coast. At the end of his sail, he and his entourage were welcomed with a celebration at a Miami park. A huge crowd had gathered to see the president-elect, and many prominent officials attended, including Anton Cermak, the mayor of Chicago.

After Roosevelt spoke briefly to the crowd from the back of his convertible car, Cermak moved through the group around Roosevelt to shake his hand and talk. Suddenly there was a popping noise, like the sound of a car backfiring or a firecracker exploding. Shouts and screams followed, and then the driver of Roosevelt's car revved his motor. Roosevelt realized that Cermak was being held up by one of his aides and had blood leaking out on the front of his shirt. Someone in the crowd had been shooting at them.

Roosevelt ordered that Cermak be put into the car and then held him close all the way to the hospital. At first, Roosevelt believed Cermak was dead, but later the injured mayor began to breathe more strongly. Showing no signs of fear or hesitation, Roosevelt had remained completely alert and calm while others around him were near hysteria.

The gunman was Giuseppe Zangara, who had immigrated from Italy in 1923. Zangara was arrested at the park immediately after the shooting. Clearly, he had been aiming to shoot Roosevelt, not Cermak. Friendless and unemployed, Zangara had suffered for many years from ill health. He confessed to a lifelong hatred of all public officials, prime ministers, presidents, kings. Cermak eventually died, and Zangara was later executed in the electric chair for his crime.

Shock engulfed the nation, but Roosevelt seemed unshaken by his brush with death and refused to cut back on public appearances. The press found him vigorous and confident. His courage inspired Americans who had spent so many long, hard months in despair over the Depression.

Finally, Inauguration Day arrived, a cold and raw Saturday, March 4, 1933. As he approached his task, Roosevelt seemed serious and determined to those around him. In the morning he and Cabinet members and their families met at St. John's Episcopal Church across the street from the White House, where Endicott Peabody, Roosevelt's old headmaster from Groton, conducted a service. Peabody prayed for grace and help for "Thy servant, Franklin, about to become President of these United States."

"We were Catholics, Protestants, Jews," said Frances Perkins, the new secretary of labor, "but I doubt that anyone remembered the difference." [1]

"First of all," Roosevelt told the crowd at his inaugural, "let me assert my firm belief that the only thing we have to fear is fear itself—nameless, unreasoning, unjustified terror."

He closed his speech by calling for divine guidance:

"In this dedication of a Nation we humbly ask the blessing of God. May He protect each and every one of us. May He guide me in the days to come."[2]

Almost immediately, Roosevelt set to work with the Cabinet: Cordell Hull, secretary of state; William Woodin, secretary of the treasury; Harold Ickes, secretary of the interior; Henry Wallace, secretary of agriculture; Frances Perkins, secretary of labor; Homer Cummings, attorney general; Daniel Roper, secretary of commerce; and James Farley, postmaster general.

Hundreds of other people were soon flooding into Washington to help with the task of trying to get the nation back on its feet. Many of these New Dealers and brain trusters were lawyers, college professors, and social workers—people who had never before had a role in the federal government. They were far younger and much more liberal than those who had surrounded Hoover. Some had even been socialists; some had been interested in communism. They brought new ideas and a sense of excitement that the capital had not seen in some time.

Each day began in much the same way for Roosevelt. He woke up at eight A.M. for breakfast in bed and looked through the major newspapers. At nine his secretaries and aides and usually Louis Howe came to discuss his day's schedule with him. While he dressed and shaved with the help of a valet, he often talked business with a Cabinet member. By ten-thirty he was pushed in his wheelchair to the Oval Office, where he spent the rest of the day—often eating lunch at his desk. Throughout the day the stream of visitors, phone calls, and memos never stopped.

Roosevelt did not attack the problems before him on a strictly intellectual basis, although he was a man of high intelligence, according to Frances Perkins. He liked to apply feeling and emotions to problems as well as logic and argument. "His emotions, his intuitive understanding, his imagination, his moral and traditional bias, his sense of right and wrong—all entered into his thinking," she found.[3]

As Roosevelt took office there was the feeling that if he could not bring change quickly, the nation might fall prey to political upheaval—perhaps even communism. On the far left were several political groups demanding immediate help for the lower classes. A Long Beach, California, doctor, Francis Townsend, led a group that proposed that every retired person over sixty receive a pension of $200 a month. He believed that the money these elderly would spend would help put the nation on the road to recovery. The Reverend Charles Coughlin of Detroit, a popular radio speaker, attacked the banking system over the airways and argued that a silver-based monetary system would solve the nation's ills. The Louisiana senator Huey Long had launched the Share Our Wealth program, calling for liquidation of all fortunes above a certain amount. Long wanted every family to have a home, a car, and a radio and urged free college educations, and pensions for the elderly.

With all this pressure in the background, Roosevelt took on his first major crisis—the need to salvage the nation's feeble banking system. Beginning in February 1933, several states had to declare bank holidays, the closing of banks for several days, to stop the run on deposits. Everywhere, anxious bank customers stood in long lines with bags and suitcases to carry away the money and gold they had deposited. By the time of Roosevelt's inauguration, thirty-eight states had temporarily closed their banks and the nation's gold reserves were dwindling.

On his first night in office, Roosevelt set the new secretary of the treasury, William Woodin, to work on an emergency banking bill. The next day Roosevelt called a special session of Congress for March 9 to consider Woodin's bill. He also declared a week-long national bank holiday and stopped transactions in gold.

Working around the clock, Woodin's Treasury Department came up with a bill calling for issuing Federal Reserve notes to help ease the crisis. The bill also called for reopening banks that were solvent and for reorganizing the rest. It gave official permission to Roosevelt to control movements of gold. Although some had thought Roosevelt might even nationalize, or take complete control of, the banks, he stopped far short of that. Although he was a liberal who favored taking action in a crisis, he wanted to move moderately in the beginning in order to build national unity. Later his reforms would become more radical.

The banking bill, called the Emergency Banking Act, was sent to Congress with portions simply penciled in. In the House there was only one copy, and the Speaker had to read it to members. Even so, the anxious congressmen worked speedily through the document and in less than eight hours it went to Roosevelt to be signed. Soon money and gold were flowing back into the banks. Roosevelt had faced his first crisis and won. Congress, which had fought so bitterly against the leadership of Herbert Hoover, seemed ready to do whatever Roosevelt wanted.

Roosevelt also excelled in handling the public. At his first press conference, he told reporters he wanted a more friendly, open atmosphere. Hoover had often sent spokesmen to talk to the press. But Roosevelt proposed meeting with reporters himself on Tuesdays and Fridays. In his first term he held 337 press conferences. News people jammed the Oval Office, where he sat at his desk and answered questions. He loved joking with reporters and hearing what they thought of his ideas.

On Sunday evening, March 12, he held the first of his "fireside chats," a series of speeches broadcast on the radio to the nation. He explained the banking situation in clear, easy-to-understand terms. Just the tone of his voice made his listeners believe that he was in control of the crisis. Although he sat at a desk in the diplomatic reception room while he gave these radio talks, he wanted to give Americans the feeling that he was at home with them in their living rooms, and to a large extent he succeeded.

"Let us unite in banishing fear," he said in his first

fireside chat. "It is your problem no less than it is mine. Together we cannot fail."[4]

But the banking bill was only the start. Because he had called in Congress for a special session, Roosevelt had more proposals. He pushed through a bill to legalize beer and wine again while the various states were repealing Prohibition. He also still believed that the federal government had to be cautious about spending, and he convinced Congress to pass a government economy bill that allowed him to cut federal salaries by $100 million and to trim $400 million from payments to veterans. These economy measures in some ways seemed to be conservative programs that were out of line with what Roosevelt wanted to accomplish, but Roosevelt and many of his advisers sincerely believed that the Hoover administration had been spending wildly and lavishly before leaving office. If the budget were not cut, taxes would have to be raised.

These early days of Roosevelt's administration came to be called the Hundred Days, a period when Roosevelt pushed fifteen major new laws through Congress. The nation had never seen anything like it before. At times in the past, critics had believed that Roosevelt lacked strength of character and had few ideas about what action to take. But after his inauguration he became confident and aggressive, taking charge of Congress like a general marshaling his army. What little opposition there was to his ideas on Capitol Hill seemed to melt away.

Some new bills passed called for the federal government to assume powers it had never had before. Not everyone, even among Roosevelt's staff, believed that these powers were provided for in the Constitution and that the federal government was acting legally. But it was an emergency, and in time of emergency extraordinary measures must be taken, Roosevelt's advisers believed.

Among the first actions was help for the nation's farmers, who had seen the prices for their crops drop by more than 50 percent in three years. But their mortgage payments were not dropping, and thousands of farmers were being evicted from their homes as banks foreclosed on their property. It seemed vital that farmers cut down on the acres they planted so that prices would go up, but how to get them to do that?

The result was a package of farm legislation including the Agricultural Adjustment Act, which called for the government to lease farmland and withdraw it from cultivation and to delay the marketing of surplus crops and even to buy up some crops. All of this was to be paid for by a tax on processors of farm products: the millers who handled corn and wheat, the cotton brokers, the textile manufacturers. A new agency was also founded, the Farm Credit Administration, that refinanced farm mortgages so that farmers would not lose their property to banks.

Some of the early methods used were upsetting to many Americans. In 1933 hundreds of thousands of farmers were persuaded to plow under their cotton in return for a hundred million dollars in benefit payments. The outcry grew louder when the government decided to buy and slaughter 5 or 6 million baby pigs before they could grow to full size and glut the market for pork. Republicans particularly were outraged. How could the government destroy all this production of American agriculture when millions did not have proper clothing or food? It didn't seem to matter that most of the baby pigs were used as fertilizer or were eventually eaten by someone.

"We must play with the cards that are dealt," Secretary of Agriculture Henry Wallace told critics. "Agriculture cannot survive in a capitalistic society as a philanthropic enterprise."[5]

Limiting farm production was a way of pushing up prices, a way of creating inflation. In future decades in America the pressure focused on controlling prices and stopping inflation. But in the Great Depression era, many saw inflation as a key way to improve the economy. Prices and wages needed to go up, not down, some of Roose-

116

velt's advisers argued. The value of the dollar had to be cheapened. One way to do this was to take the dollar off the international gold standard, an action that Roosevelt also took during the first Hundred Days. No longer did the government have to pledge to back up its dollars in a specific amount of gold. Roosevelt's conservative advisers, many of whom feared runaway inflation, were horrified. "This is the end of western civilization," Roosevelt's budget director, Lewis Douglas, said.[6]

But Roosevelt was willing to try new ideas, no matter how controversial, to turn America around. In the past many of the decisions about the nation's financial system were set by bankers on Wall Street, who were not accountable to the public. But under Roosevelt's new gold policy, the federal government had more control over how much inflation there would be and what the interest rates would be for savers and borrowers.

Other measures passed during the Hundred Days included establishment of the Civilian Conservation Corps, government-paid crews who planted trees, built reservoirs and bridges, restored historic landmarks, and set up beaches and campgrounds. Eventually, more than 2.5 million men between the ages of eighteen and twenty-five found work in the corps. Many came out of the slums and ghettos of America and had never seen forests or mountains before. Most stayed in the CCC camps for six months to a year and gained job skills that changed their lives.

Although many new measures spent federal money, Roosevelt in these early days still aimed to balance the budget, as did his budget director, Lewis Douglas. New taxes were supposed to pay many of the bills. Once built, building projects were supposed to pay for themselves by bringing in revenue. Typical of this sort of project was the Tennessee Valley Authority, set up by an act of Congress in May 1933. The TVA's purpose was to build dams and power plants along the Tennessee River to benefit the poor farming areas of several Southern states. Electric power and fertilizers were produced and sold, forests were re-planted, and eroded land was restored.

During the first Hundred Days there was also the Truth-in-Securities Act, requiring full disclosure when new securities were issued, and the Home Owners' Loan Act, to refinance home mortgages.

Among the most unusual and important of the new laws was the National Industrial Recovery Act, a bill designed to stimulate recovery of the nation's factories and industries. It allowed businesses to be exempt from anti-trust laws in order to draft agreements about prices and competition, it provided for government licensing of businesses, and it guaranteed the right of collective bargaining to labor. It also provided $3.3 billion for public works projects. The idea was that those employed in public works would earn money to buy the goods available from the expansion of business. Because labor unions had new power to bargain with management, they would be more successful in getting higher wages for workers. Roosevelt and his advisers believed that with fatter paychecks workers would spend more and thus boost the economy. In a sense the bill aimed to create a minitrust in every industry to relieve competition and thereby allow for higher prices and wages.

The bill was introduced in June and passed in less than a week even though some argued that it would allow businesses to engage in price fixing. But Roosevelt firmly believed the bill would put people back to work. "It is a challenge to industry," he said, "which has long insisted that, given the right to act in unison, it could do much for the general good which has hitherto been unlawful. From today it has that right." [7]

Many ideas for this legislation had come from General Hugh Johnson, a former Army man and a member of Roosevelt's brain trust, who had been part of the group that had helped Roosevelt in his presidential campaign.

After the bill passed, Roosevelt appointed Johnson to head the new National Recovery Administration (NRA).

But Johnson was too volatile a personality to handle the public works program as well, Roosevelt believed. So those projects were assigned to Harold Ickes in the Department of the Interior—to Johnson's great dissatisfaction. Johnson believed that the two programs had to be under single leadership, that the public works contracts should be awarded only to those willing to cooperate on wages and hours and prices. He was ready to resign but eventually was persuaded to stay. But it was the beginning of a rocky and tempestuous period. The NRA went on to create much controversy in the Roosevelt administration.

Johnson viewed his job as one of persuading businesses to voluntarily agree to shorter hours, higher wages, and better trade practices in code hearings which he held with various industrial groups. He persuaded the cotton textile industry to end its use of child labor. Some codes set floors on prices to prevent price wars aimed at driving competition out of business; others tried to prevent businesses from selling cheap and shoddy merchandise. But often the codes were complex and silly, like a rule against selling egg noodles in yellow cellophane because it might make them look richer and more delicious than they actually were.

Soon Johnson launched a nationwide campaign to get all employers to pay a minimum of $12 or $13 a week for forty hours of work. As a reward, businesses could use a special symbol, the Blue Eagle, with the slogan, "We do our part." Industry group after industry group joined the crusade. It was the domestic equivalent of a war campaign, but instead of fighting a human enemy, the nation was fighting the Depression.

It was all done on a voluntary basis, with public opinion as the only weapon to use against code violators. But by the fall of 1933, the campaign was arousing controversy. Businesses were angry that they could not raise prices enough to go along with the higher wages; they felt that labor was getting too powerful. Meanwhile, workers claimed that the new codes were being ignored and that the NRA was too weak to enforce them. Others claimed that the NRA's methods bordered on socialism and dictatorship. Even some inside the administration told Roosevelt to abolish the NRA, but he still supported the program.

All these programs were aimed at pushing the economy to right itself, but Roosevelt also wanted to give direct relief to Americans in need—money and help for those who could not wait until new jobs opened up. In many cases, state and local relief programs were bankrupt and had nothing left to give to the poor.

Harry Hopkins, who had worked for Roosevelt in a relief agency in New York, brought the president a proposal for a federal relief program that would grant money directly to states. Soon the Federal Emergency Relief Administration was created, with authority to grant $500 million in aid.

When the bill went to the Senate in March, there were again complaints. "It is socialism," said one congressman. "Whether it is communism or not I do not know."[8]

But the bill easily passed both houses, and Hopkins became administrator of the new agency. By the second day after passage of the bill, Hopkins had a staff, had notified state governors that they needed to set up organizations to handle the money, and had sent emergency grants to seven states.

Although some of the money was given as grants to the needy, Hopkins felt that taking money could destroy a person's morale, that the recipient should perform some service in return. So states created work-relief projects to hire those getting aid.

Because Ickes had been slow to launch the Public Works Administration, Hopkins was also given some PWA money to use in a federal work program known as the Civil Works Administration. By January 1934 he had 4 million people working in CWA programs: building roads and highways and schools, developing parks, and digging swimming pools and sewers.

Although some contended that the jobs and money were going to people too lazy to find work on their own, relief officials contended that many recipients were unemployed people who had lived as long as they could on their savings and finally had to go on relief or face starvation.

In the South, white planters who had depended on black laborers for decades complained that blacks would no longer work for low wages. The governor of Georgia passed on to Roosevelt a letter from a farmer who complained: "I wouldn't plow nobody's mule from sunrise to sunset for 50 cents per day when I could get $1.30 for pretending to work on a ditch."

Roosevelt replied: "I take it, from your sending the letter of the gentleman from Smithville to me that you approve of paying farm labor 40 to 50 cents per day . . . Somehow I cannot get it into my head that wages on such a scale make possible a reasonable American standard of living." [9]

Even so, Roosevelt faced pressure from some in the administration who felt that the Civil Works Administration program was too expensive and must end. There had also been waste and corruption in the program.

So although Roosevelt was deluged by letters and demonstrations supporting CWA, the program was largely shut down in 1934.

12

"I never knew him to face life . . . with fear"

The economy took a brief spurt forward after Roosevelt's inauguration but then began to sputter in late 1933 and in 1934. The National Recovery Administration had run into problems in trying to spur business recovery; crop cutbacks arranged by the Agricultural Adjustment Administration seemed to take effect very slowly. In late 1934 the unemployment rate was still extraordinarily high, an estimated 17 percent, and national income for 1934 totaled $10 billion less than it had in 1931. Roosevelt, who had seemed like a miracle worker during the first Hundred Days, faced new criticism from those on the left, including Huey Long and Father Coughlin, and those on the right—business people, Republicans, and conservative Democrats.

In August 1934 a new organization had even formed known as the American Liberty League, made up of those who contended America would become a welfare state under Roosevelt. Among its founders were old Roosevelt opponents—Al Smith, Jouett Shouse, and John J. Raskob.

That is not to say that Roosevelt had done nothing since the end of the Hundred Days. Since that first honeymoon with Congress, more new legislation had come out of Washington, including a bill signed in June 1934 that created the Securities and Exchange Commission to provide for tougher regulation of stocks and bonds sold on Wall Street. Wealthy investor Joseph P. Kennedy, whose son John would one day become president, was chosen to head the commission.

By the fall of 1934, however, Roosevelt had concluded that regulation of business might not be enough to push the economy forward. He also began to believe recovery might not be possible if he insisted on a balanced federal budget. To help the poor and unemployed, deficit spending might be necessary.

What he came up with was the Works Progress Administration, a giant plan for publicly funded jobs aimed at employing 3½ million people. Eventually, Congress gave Roosevelt power to spend $5 billion on this program of work relief. Harold Ickes and Harry Hopkins battled over who would control the money. Ickes favored using it for large-scale public building projects of the type he was planning in the Public Works Administration. But Hopkins pushed for smaller-scale projects to put as many people to work as possible as soon as possible. Hopkins eventually won out, although there were still major grants to the Public Works Administration, which, besides building schools, courthouses, and city halls, helped build dams, bridges, aircraft carriers, and military airports.

The Works Progress Administration built and remodeled some 5,900 schools, 2,500 hospitals, 1,000 airplane landing fields, and 13,000 playgrounds. It also funded the Federal Theatre Project, which produced plays and shows and hired unemployed actors and other theater people. Artists were employed to paint murals and give arts and crafts classes. Scholars collected the oral histories of older Americans, including the memoirs of former slaves who were still alive in the 1930s. Musicians performed concerts. The Federal Writers' Project wrote dozens of guides to cities, states, and regions around the country and wrote 150 books in a special "Life in America" series. A National Youth Administration found jobs for college students.

The 1934 elections were an important test for Roosevelt. Usually in the off-year congressional elections, the party in control of the White House loses ground. Most Democrats had estimated that they would lose thirty or forty seats in the House of Representatives. But instead of picking up seats, the Republicans lost thirteen. Republican membership in the House fell to its lowest point in history. In the Senate the Democrats had won a two-thirds majority and had sixty-nine seats.

The victory was a tribute to Roosevelt's popularity. No matter what his failings, Americans saw him as the man who could save the nation. During his administration some 5,000 to 8,000 letters a day poured into the White House, many from jobless and troubled Americans seeking help. In the summer of 1934 Roosevelt had taken a train trip across country. At every little stop on the way, thousands turned out to wave and get a glimpse of him. "Coming across the continent the reception was grand," Roosevelt told Vice President Garner, "and I am more than ever convinced that, so far as having the people with us goes, we are just as strong—perhaps stronger—than ever before."[1]

What may have made people love Roosevelt so much, said his wife, Eleanor, was that he never believed that there was a problem too big for human beings to solve. "I never knew him to face life or any problem that came up with fear," she said.[2]

In 1935 Congress passed several other bills proposed by Roosevelt in a new wave of legislation that some have called the second Hundred Days or Second New Deal. Many writers and historians believe that under pressure from political forces on the left, Roosevelt pushed for reforms that

124

called for stronger action by government and that were aimed at aiding the poor and dispossessed.

One measure he sought in the spring of 1935 was a plan for old-age insurance, a social security system. A special Committee on Economic Security, headed by Frances Perkins, the secretary of labor, studied the pension question and developed the Social Security Act, which proposed plans for old-age pensions and an unemployment compensation system, to provide payments for unemployed workers. The pensions for those sixty-five and older were to be funded by taxing employers and people who were still working. It was to be largely a federal program. The unemployment system, also funded by taxing workers and employers, was to be a joint state-federal program. Hearings began in January but dragged on because of heavy opposition in Congress even though old-age insurance and unemployment payments had been part of the Democratic party platform in 1932.

Some business leaders prophesied that unemployment insurance would set the nation on the road to socialism. Why would anyone work if they could collect money for not working? Why would anyone save for the future if they thought they could collect a pension automatically after they retired? "Industry has every reason to be alarmed at the social, economic and financial implications," said Alfred Sloan of General Motors. "The dangers are manifest."[3]

But there was also pressure from the followers of Dr. Townsend, the California physician who was promoting pensions for the elderly. His organization complained that the proposed pensions were far too small.

Finally, by June, the bill had passed both houses of Congress, and Roosevelt signed it into law in August. "[Roosevelt] always regarded the Social Security Act as the cornerstone of his administration," said Frances Perkins, "and, I think, took greater satisfaction from it than from anything else he achieved on the domestic front."[4]

NEW DEAL AGENCIES

Franklin Roosevelt was responsible for tremendous growth in the size and complexity of the federal government. Here is a list of some agencies that began under his administration with a brief description of their work.

Agricultural Adjustment Administration (AAA)—set up in 1933; launched an era in which American farmers received aid from the federal government. This agency gave benefit payments to farmers who cut back on growing basic crops such as wheat, corn, and cotton.

Civilian Conservation Corps (CCC)—established in 1933; hired jobless young men from poor families to work on reforestation and soil conservation and other projects.

Civil Works Administration (CWA)—during the bleakest winter of the Depression, 1933–34, hired 4 million people to build schools, playgrounds, airports, and other projects. The agency went out of business in the spring of 1934.

Fair Employment Practices Commission (FEPC)—organized in 1941; worked to ensure that wartime industries did not discriminate in hiring based on religion, race, or ethnic background.

Farm Credit Administration (FCA)—created in 1933, refinanced farm mortgages so that banks would not foreclose on farmers' land.

Federal Deposit Insurance Corporation (FDIC)—still in existence today; created in 1933 as an insurance system to guarantee the safety of bank deposits.

Federal Emergency Relief Administration (FERA)—set up in 1933; channeled federal relief money to state and local agencies.

Federal Housing Administration (FHA)—created in 1934; insured home mortgages.

National Labor Relations Board (NLRB)—created in 1935 by the National Labor Relations, or

Wagner, Act to give federal protection to collective bargaining and to prevent unfair practices by employers.

National Recovery Administration (NRA)—set up in 1933; gave federal protection to businesses that wanted to enter into agreements to stabilize prices and production. The agency also pushed for fair wages and hours for workers. It went out of business after the Supreme Court ruled its system of codes invalid in 1935.

National War Labor Board (NWLB)—created during World War II to help settle strikes and labor disputes and to set wages.

National Youth Administration (NYA)—organized in 1935; found part-time jobs for college and high school students.

Office of Economic Stabilization (OES)—created during World War II; worked to hold down inflation in prices, profits, and wages.

Office of Price Administration (OPA)—worked to control prices during World War II.

Public Works Administration (PWA)—set up in 1933; financed large-scale public works projects as a way of increasing employment and consumer buying power.

Securities and Exchange Commission (SEC)—established in 1934 to investigate the worth of new stocks and securities and to police the stock market.

Social Security System—set up in 1935 to provide federal pensions and aid payments to the aged and disabled.

Tennessee Valley Authority (TVA)—created in 1933 to build dams on the Tennessee River to provide flood control, generate cheap electricity, and revitalize a poverty-stricken region.

Works Progress Administration (WPA)—established as an emergency federal job program in 1935; designed to replace direct relief payments with "work relief."

From the beginning of the New Deal, Roosevelt and his advisers had worried about how the Supreme Court would react to the sweeping reforms that they had made. At the time, the Court was composed of four conservative-minded justices: Pierce Butler, James McReynolds, George Sutherland, and Willis Van Devanter; three who were considered liberals: Louis Brandeis, Benjamin Cardozo, and Harlan Fiske Stone; and two who were considered middle-of-the-road in their thinking: Chief Justice Charles Evans Hughes and Owen Roberts.

It took awhile before any major piece of New Deal legislation reached the Supreme Court. The first was the National Industrial Recovery Act. On May 27, 1935, a day the New Dealers later labeled as "Black Monday," the Court voted 9–0 to strike down the act.

The ruling came in what was known as the "sick chicken" case, involving some Brooklyn, New York, poultry dealers, the Schechter brothers. They had been convicted of violating the poultry code of the National Recovery Administration by selling diseased chickens and not paying wages as set by the code. The federal government had no authority to regulate the Schechters, the Court said, because their business was not part of interstate commerce. Worse yet for the New Dealers, Chief Justice Hughes said that the codes set up by Roosevelt's administration were an "unconstitutional delegation of legislative power."[5] Suddenly, the NRA codes for businesses and the provisions to help labor were dead.

Although Roosevelt was devastated, he at first said very little publicly about the decision. Thousands of telegrams and letters were pouring into the White House from people whose wages were cut and whose hours were changed due to the decision. Then on May 31 he lashed out at the Court in a press conference: "Are the people of this country going to decide that their Federal Government shall in the future have no right under any implied power to enter into a national economic problem?" He added:

"We have been relegated to the horse-and-buggy definition of interstate commerce."[6]

The Court decision seemed to give Roosevelt new energy. Before Congress went home that summer he pushed lawmakers to pass a number of bills, including some that had been creeping along for months. Among them was Senator Robert Wagner's National Labor Relations bill, which organized labor had long supported. Roosevelt had long been lukewarm about this bill because he believed that the NRA could provide the kinds of wage and hour guarantees that labor wanted. But once the NRA was dead, Roosevelt began to speak up for the Wagner bill. Finally passed in late June, the bill became one of the most important pieces of legislation to come out of the New Deal. It gave federal support to the right of labor to organize employees and bargain with bosses. It also set up a National Labor Relations Board to enforce the measures of the bill. It forbade some so-called unfair practices that businesses had used against unions. The bill allowed for tremendous growth in the membership of unions and helped cement Roosevelt's strong support from laborers.

On June 19 Roosevelt also came out with a far-reaching proposal for new inheritance taxes, gift taxes, and graduated taxes for the wealthy and big businesses. In its final version the Wealth Tax Act was not nearly as far-reaching as first proposed. But it did satisfy in part some of the followers of Huey Long while it stirred up new resentment among businesses and the upper classes.

Also that summer, Roosevelt pushed through a measure to break up the large holding companies which controlled electric power utilities throughout the country. They often overcharged consumers and managed to evade state regulation. An early version of the bill gave the Securities and Exchange Commission the power to dissolve any utility holding company which could not justify its existence. This "death sentence" sparked heavy opposition from utility company lobbyists and eventually had to be removed from the bill. But the final law did break up most of the largest utility empires within three years and provided for close scrutiny over power company finances.

Yet another law that came out of Congress that summer was the Banking Act, which strengthened the Federal Reserve System's control over the nation's banks.

Throughout all this, the nation observed a very different White House than the past few presidents had had. Under Roosevelt it became a casual and friendly place that sometimes seemed like a boardinghouse because of all the guests it housed. Louis Howe and Missy LeHand lived there, as did various Roosevelt children and their spouses and the Roosevelt grandchildren. Sara Roosevelt was also a frequent resident. And, of course, there were the formal visits of prime ministers and high officials of other nations. There were lots of parties, warmth, and laughter. Often traditions and rules were shattered by rambunctious and exuberant Roosevelts.

The First Lady shocked the White House staff by insisting on running the elevator herself without the aid of a doorman. And once, one of the Roosevelt sons returned late at night from a party in a beat-up car and had a tough time convincing the guards at the gate that he should be let into the White House. "What kind of a place is this anyway where you can't get in when you are living here?" he said angrily the next morning.[7]

The White House staff was not especially well managed by Eleanor Roosevelt, who was more interested in world affairs and politics than in how maids dusted the furniture or what cooks put on the table. She had brought a former Hyde Park neighbor, Henrietta Nesbitt, to Washington to manage the housekeeping staff.

Franklin Roosevelt disliked this woman, but Eleanor staunchly defended her. At elegant parties, for example, Mrs. Nesbitt might serve mutton and boiled carrots, washed down with mediocre wines. Roosevelt once sent his wife a nasty memo to complain about eating chicken six times in one week followed by sweetbreads, or calf thymus, another six times.

At first, Eleanor had reluctantly taken on the job of First Lady. Shortly after her husband had been nominated, she had written a letter to a close woman friend expressing her doubts and fears about living in the White House. The friend went to Louis Howe for advice and showed him the letter. Howe destroyed it for fear it might become public. "From the personal standpoint, I did not want my husband to be president," Eleanor later wrote. "It was pure selfishness on my part, and I never mentioned my feelings on the subject to him."[8]

Eleanor believed the presidency would infringe on her personal life and dearly won independence. But she quickly became an effective aide to her husband in his job. She traveled to places that were hard for him to reach due to his physical handicap. She became his eyes and ears and provided him with information for making decisions.

Often she took on controversial situations for him. In March 1933, protesting World War I veterans marched on Washington to demand payment of a wartime service bonus that they were supposed to get in 1945. The same thing had happened in 1932, under President Hoover, and Hoover had sent in the Army to drive the bonus marchers out of a ramshackle camp built on the Anacostia River. But Roosevelt allowed the bonus marchers in 1933 to use an old campground, where they were fed for free. Eleanor visited them, made a lunchtime speech, and toured several of their buildings.

"Often people came to me to enlist his [Roosevelt's] support for an idea," she said. "Although I might present the situation to him, I never urged on him a specific course of action, no matter how strongly I felt, because I realized he knew of factors in the picture as a whole of which I might be ignorant."[9]

Eleanor was particularly concerned about the problems of the nation's African-Americans. She brought Walter White, secretary of the National Association for the Advancement of Colored People, to Roosevelt to urge passage of an antilynching bill designed to stop the brutal mob killings of blacks in the South. The president denounced lynching but was reluctant to push hard for an antilynching bill for fear of alienating the white Southern congressmen whose votes he needed to pass his economic reform measures.

When Eleanor asked him if she could speak out strongly on the question, he gave his approval. "You can say anything you want. I can always say, 'Well, that is my wife; I can't do anything about her.' "[10]

The antilynching bill never passed Congress, but increasing discussion of the problem led several states to pass such bills of their own.

Although blacks often criticized Roosevelt for not taking more vigorous action on civil rights, they were pleased that he appointed blacks to important government posts and were impressed with Eleanor Roosevelt's efforts.

But as the national spotlight fell on Eleanor and the Roosevelt children, they were often criticized for their behavior. Gossip and rumors spread about Eleanor's close friendship with other women. Often she spent more time with them than she did with her husband and family. One of her best friends, Associated Press reporter Lorena Hickok, even moved into the White House for a while.

Roosevelt's political advisers were also upset over the divorces of the Roosevelt children Elliott, Anna, and James. "In each case Franklin had done what he could to prevent the divorce," Eleanor later commented, "but when he was convinced that the children had made up their minds after careful reflection, it never occurred to him to suggest that they should subordinate their lives to his interest."[11]

Although Eleanor and her husband worked together in the White House, their marriage still lacked warmth and affection. She never really forgave him for having been in love with Lucy Mercer many years before. At times her children observed Franklin hold out his arms to hug Eleanor, but she turned away to avoid his embrace. She was also jealous of the flirtatious friendships he sometimes had with other, more beautiful women—foreign princesses and wives of federal officials.

More controversy was stirred up during the Roosevelt administration by the president's administrative style. He surrounded himself with brilliant and hardworking people, who brought him many new ideas but also competed among themselves for his support and attention. Instead of smoothing the waters, he seemed to encourage the upheaval by teasing and manipulating his associates. Secretary of State Cordell Hull said, "He gave the impression almost of being a spectator looking on and enjoying the drama." [12]

Still he was intensely loyal and concerned about others. He became very distressed when anyone tried to resign and could scarcely bear to fire anyone. According to historian Arthur M. Schlesinger, Jr., "The competitive approach to administration gave Roosevelt great advantages. It brought him an effective flow of information; it kept the reins of decision in his own hands; it made for administrative flexibility and stimulated subordinates to effective performance." [13]

13

"This generation . . . has a rendezvous with destiny"

Franklin Roosevelt's problems with the Supreme Court had only begun with the "sick chicken" case in 1935. Early in 1936 the court ruled 6–3 that the tax imposed on food processors and brokers to pay for the work of the Agricultural Adjustment Administration (AAA) was unconstitutional. The Court even ordered the return of $200 million already collected from processors, such as cotton gins and flour mills.

The decision threatened Roosevelt's attempts to pay for his new programs and balance the budget. It also threatened the efforts to get farmers to control the size of their crops. Farm prices immediately began to decline.

Because the Court rulings had killed the AAA, New Deal officials came up with a new farm law, the Soil Conservation and Domestic Allotment Act, that paid farmers not to plant crops that depleted the soil of nutrients. It was a law aimed at reducing overproduction and at improving the fertility of the soil.

Many months before the 1936 presidential election, Roosevelt had begun his campaign for a second term with

134

a series of "nonpolitical" trips and speeches. He was just performing his duties as president, but clearly he was on the campaign trail. He startled Congress in January by breaking with tradition and appearing at an evening session to deliver his State of the Union message. The speech was broadcast on the radio as well.

As he faced this second campaign for the White House, Roosevelt no longer had the help of his longtime aide, Louis Howe. In early 1935 Howe's lung problems confined him to his bed in the White House, where he spent much of his time gasping for air in an oxygen tent. Eleanor Roosevelt closely supervised his care and tried to reassure him that he would soon be well enough to join the 1936 campaign. But by the spring of 1936 he had to be moved to Washington's Naval Hospital, and on April 18 he died.

His illness and death left a gap in her husband's life, Eleanor believed, and Roosevelt kept trying to fill it with new associates who never quite met the challenge. "For one reason and another, no one quite filled the void which unconsciously he was seeking to fill, and each one in turn disappeared from the scene, occasionally with a bitterness which I understood but always regretted," she said.[1]

To some extent Roosevelt filled the void by depending more on Eleanor's advice and on a growing friendship with Harry Hopkins, chief of the Works Progress Administration.

In June the Republicans held their convention in Cleveland, Ohio, and nominated a progressive candidate, Alf Landon, the Republican governor of Kansas. Landon was a poor public speaker, but he was steady and comfortable and down-to-earth—just the sort of person, Republicans thought, who could show up the sophisticated and worldly Roosevelt. Landon promised to balance the budget but also said he would not throw out the New Deal economic reforms. Wealthy people, who were terrified of Roosevelt's taxation policies, and major business executives, upset with the new controls over industry and banks, poured money into Landon's campaign coffers. And a number of prominent Democrats, including Al Smith and John W. Davis, both former presidential nominees, bolted their party to back Landon.

Republicans had hoped that Roosevelt would lose votes in 1936 to Louisiana senator Huey Long, who was thinking about making a presidential bid. But Long was assassinated by a gunman in the Louisiana State House in September 1935. Followers of Long, allied with Dr. Townsend and Father Coughlin, still tried to organize a third-party presidential ticket, but their organization, the National Union for Social Justice, attracted few voters and had little effect on the election.

After Roosevelt and Garner were renominated by the Democrats, Roosevelt announced his acceptance in one of his most famous speeches, given before a crowd of over a hundred thousand at Franklin Field in Philadelphia. He lashed out at the forces of big business: "These economic royalists complain that we seek to overthrow the institutions of America. What they really complain of is that we seek to take away their power . . . In vain they seek to hide behind the Flag and the Constitution."

Near the end he said, "There is a mysterious cycle in human events. To some generations much is given. Of other generations much is expected. This generation of Americans has a rendezvous with destiny." [2]

Wild cheers and applause thundered on from the crowd as Roosevelt circled the stadium field in a car.

Although Landon ran a smooth and well-financed campaign, polls showed Roosevelt running ahead of the Kansas governor. Gradually, the Republicans stepped up their criticism, charging that Roosevelt was becoming a dictator who would attempt to tamper with the makeup of the Supreme Court in order to get what he wanted.

In his final speech of the campaign, at Madison Square Garden in New York City, Roosevelt lashed back at his critics. He said that before he was elected, "For twelve years this Nation was afflicted with hear-nothing, see-nothing, do-nothing Government." By contrast, in his first administration, "the forces of selfishness and of lust for power met their match."[3]

On Election Day Roosevelt sat in the dining room of the family home at Hyde Park and watched the teletype machines and a large chart where a tally was kept of the vote. He ended up with a massive victory, winning every state except for Maine and Vermont. "I knew I should have gone to Maine and Vermont," he joked, "but Jim [Farley] wouldn't let me."[4]

Roosevelt believed that the 1936 election had given him a mandate to take even bolder steps as president. He wanted to push Congress to reorganize the executive branch of government. He also still aimed to help the unemployed and needy, and he believed that he could not effectively change America's economic structure without changing its court system. Conservatives dominated the Supreme Court, and he believed that as long as they did so, they would make it difficult to push forward economic reforms.

Some in America viewed the Supreme Court as an almost sacred institution above the give-and-take of political life. However, as Roosevelt saw it, the justices were appointed by presidents who had politics in mind when they made their choices. The High Court was involved in politics, he believed, just as the Congress and the president were.

In his 1937 inaugural address he referred to the problems he had with the Court's interpretation of the Constitution, an interpretation which he found rigid and which had hampered his legislative program. "The Constitution of 1787 did not make our democracy impotent," he said.

Much work remained to be done as part of the New Deal, he said. "I see one-third of the nation ill-housed, ill-clad, ill-nourished."[5]

He believed that to deal with these problems the Constitution had to be a flexible document, one that would

137

shift slightly so the nation could make progress in the modern world. He believed that most Americans shared this view, and that the Supreme Court and the lower federal courts had to respond to this situation.

So behind the scenes, Roosevelt worked with the Department of Justice on a plan to revamp the Supreme Court. In February 1937 he sent his Court proposal to Congress with almost no advance warning. The lawmakers were shocked with what he wanted. The problem was, he said, that the federal courts were overloaded and even the Supreme Court could not handle the workload of cases. This was partly due, he said, to the fact that many judges were "aged or infirm."[6] He recommended that when a federal judge who had served at least ten years did not retire within six months after he or she turned seventy, the president should be able to add a new judge to the bench. There would be limits though. No more than six new justices could be added to the Supreme Court and no more than forty-four new judges to lower federal courts.

Roosevelt told Congress: "Modern complexities call also for a constant infusion of new blood in the courts, just as it is needed in executive functions of the Government and in private business. Older men, assuming that the scene is the same as it was in the past, cease to explore or inquire into the present or the future."[7]

Reaction was mixed in Congress, and few Democrats showed enthusiasm for the measure. Even Vice President Garner was critical of the bill. But Roosevelt held huge majorities in both houses of Congress, and it seemed unlikely that he could be stopped.

Conservatives announced their opposition even though they believed they were fighting a lost cause. They pointed out that the age issue was a fraudulent one, that Roosevelt was mainly aiming to change the political stand of the Court by adding new, more liberal judges. After all, one of Roosevelt's strongest supporters on the Court was the eighty-year-old, highly respected, and hardworking Louis Brandeis.

But soon, not just the conservatives were rebelling against the Court-packing plan. Many liberals and moderates joined them in an unusual alliance against the bill. Although many of these opponents were angry about the Court's recent actions, they still viewed the Supreme Court as a hallowed symbol of democracy that must be protected from any form of tampering.

What if some right-wing president came along who was just as charming and eloquent as Roosevelt and tried to change the Bill of Rights to the Constitution instead? No president, no matter how just his cause, should be allowed to manipulate the American form of government, they believed.

Newspaper editorials attacked the plan; a flood of letters of opposition swept into Congress. For the first time, Roosevelt's popularity seemed unable to assure a victory.

Then suddenly, the Supreme Court itself began to change direction, to everyone's surprise. In March, just after Senate hearings began on the Court bill, Justice Owen Roberts voted with Chief Justice Hughes and three liberal judges to uphold a state minimum-wage bill. In April the Court upheld a key piece of New Deal legislation, the National Labor Relations Act, as well. The decisions appeared to clash directly with the Court's earlier rulings throwing out New Deal measures.

Roosevelt told the press that he was jubilant. But in fact the rulings had upset his political allies who were trying to get the Court-packing plan through Congress. No one wanted to press on when it appeared that the Court was ready to do Roosevelt's bidding anyway. But the president was undaunted; he refused to back down.

New blows came in the spring. The conservative-minded Justice Van Devanter agreed to retire, making it possible for Roosevelt to appoint another, more liberal justice. Then the Supreme Court issued a favorable verdict on the Social Security Act. There seemed little left to fight for. In July the Senate majority leader, Joe Robinson, died, throwing the Roosevelt supporters into further upheaval. Robinson had been leading the fight in the Senate for the Court-packing bill.

The struggle was finally over. On July 22 the Senate voted to send the bill back to the Judiciary Committee to die a quiet death. Senator Hiram Johnson shouted, "Glory be to God!" when he heard the news.[8]

Roosevelt had paid a heavy price for his Court battle. He had thrown the Democrats into disarray and managed to give his conservative opponents a weapon to use against him for years to come. No longer would Roosevelt-sponsored legislation pass quickly through Congress with no opposition as it had in the early days of the New Deal.

On the other hand, Roosevelt had also forced the Court to change and modify its interpretation of the Constitution in line with his economic reforms. He replaced Justice Van Devanter with Senator Hugo Black of Alabama. There was some controversy over the selection because early in his career Black had belonged to the Ku Klux Klan. But Black weathered the storm and was confirmed.

Within two and a half years Roosevelt was able to name four more replacements to the Court: Stanley Reed, Felix Frankfurter, William O. Douglas, and Frank Murphy. He had turned the sometimes obstinate and balky Supreme Court into a liberal-minded Roosevelt Court.

Beginning in the summer of 1937, perhaps as an outgrowth of the upheaval of the Court-packing bill, Roosevelt faced growing opposition in Congress. A new coalition of conservative Democrats from the South united with Republicans to try to stop New Deal legislation. They were angry about government spending and labor unrest and disliked the New Deal administrators. A recession had hit the country again in late 1937 and early 1938. The president's opponents called it the "Roosevelt depression."

It was proof, they contended, that the New Deal was failing.

Many of these Democrats also feared that Roosevelt might try to run for an unprecedented third term as president in 1940, and they were determined to prevent that by wresting control of their party away from Roosevelt.

Still, in the spring of 1938, Congress agreed to Roosevelt's requests to a $3.75 billion spending program for the Public Works Administration and Works Progress Administration. Congress also agreed to fund Roosevelt's plan for a full-scale congressional inquiry into monopolies and trusts.

But a plan by Roosevelt to change and revamp some federal agencies to improve efficiency aroused strong opposition in 1938. Many in Congress contended that it was yet another attempt by Roosevelt to take power away from Congress. Some accused Roosevelt of designing to become a dictator on the order of Germany's Adolf Hitler, who was then in the process of taking over Austria. A major newspaper publisher, Frank Gannett, organized a group called the National Committee to Uphold Constitutional Government which sent 900,000 letters to Congress to protest the plan.

In the end the bill passed the Senate by a narrow margin, but lost in the House on April 8 by a vote of 204–196. It was one of Roosevelt's worst defeats in Congress, although a year later a much weaker reorganization plan would be approved.

In the spring of 1938 Congress also succeeded in greatly weakening a federal wages and hours act that decreed that within two years all workers must be paid a forty-cents-an-hour minimum wage and could work only forty hours a week. But Congress wrote so many exceptions into the bill that workers in many areas were not covered by the legislation. Among those who were unprotected were household maids and farm workers, categories which included many minority-group members.

The New Dealers were growing more and more frustrated with the opposition from lawmakers within the Democratic party. Roosevelt's adviser Harry Hopkins organized a committee to investigate ways of purging the party of some of the Democrats who kept standing in the president's way. In June 1938 Roosevelt announced in a fireside chat that he would advise citizens about which Democrat to vote for in local contests. "I have every right to speak in those few instances where there may be a clear issue between candidates for a Democratic nomination," he said.[9]

He was tired of Democrats who called themselves New Dealers and Roosevelt supporters but who, after they got elected, went to Congress and obstructed his programs.

Roosevelt traveled the country to endorse the candidates he favored. In some cases he succeeded, as in Kentucky, where he backed Senator Alben Barkley over his opponent Happy Chandler. But he failed to oust three Southern opponents: Walter George of Georgia, Ellison D. Smith of South Carolina, and Millard Tydings of Maryland.

The newspapers made much of the "failure" of Roosevelt's purge in these states. Then, in November, the Republicans also gained strength. Eighty new GOP members were added to the House of Representatives and eight to the Senate. Still, Democrats greatly outnumbered Republicans in both the Senate and the House.

By the fall of 1938 Roosevelt's battles with Congress were beginning to be overshadowed by events in Europe and Asia. Americans were closely watching the growing crises in other parts of the world and even picking sides in the disputes. But their memories of the bloody years of World War I were still fresh, and most were determined not to play any role in the current firestorm.

14

"We must be the great arsenal of democracy"

Even before Roosevelt took office, signs of crisis had been building in both Europe and the Far East.

During the Depression years, Japan's foreign trade had dried up as a wave of high tariffs swept the world. Inside the economically troubled country a military clique gained power. The nation's army officers believed that Japan could overcome its problems only by seizing new sources of raw materials and markets. So by 1932 Japan had overrun Manchuria and was soon pressing on to invade major cities in North China.

Many Americans believed that the United States must react to this aggression, and Roosevelt proposed slapping a trade embargo on Japan in 1933. But the isolationists in Congress protested that the United States must not get involved, and Roosevelt backed down. He did not want to fight with the Senate over Manchuria when he needed senators to work smoothly and efficiently on his New Deal legislation.

Besides, most Americans were more concerned about what was going on in Germany than they were with Japan.

Just a few weeks before Roosevelt was sworn in as president in March 1933, Nazi leader Adolf Hitler had been sworn in as chancellor of Germany.

Almost immediately, a wave of violence had been launched against Jews in Germany. Their stores were boycotted and their businesses attacked. Hundreds were beaten in violent pro-Nazi demonstrations. Official decrees barred them from enrolling in universities and from holding government jobs. In 1935 Hitler's Nuremberg Laws took away the civil rights of Jews. It was all part of the grand plan that Hitler had outlined in his book, *Mein Kampf*. The Germans were a superior race that must drive out the Jews from their empire and then take over Eastern Europe, Hitler said.

Many in the United States were shocked at this violent anti-Semitism. Through it all, Roosevelt remained silent; Secretary of State Cordell Hull insisted that the United States should not be involved with the internal politics of another country.

The violence and upheaval spread. Fascist dictator Benito Mussolini of Italy invaded Ethiopia, in North Africa, in 1935. A year later the Spanish military led by Generalissimo Francisco Franco rebelled against the leftist Republican government. The Spanish conflict grew into a bloody civil war in which Hitler and Mussolini sent men and arms to aid the right-wing Franco, who eventually triumphed.

Then, in 1936, Hitler marched his troops into the demilitarized Rhineland, a zone that had been created as part of the Treaty of Versailles that ended World War I. The treaty had also put strict limits on Germany's armed forces, but Hitler began rearming the nation.

Although Americans feared the threats overseas, most firmly objected to involvement in foreign wars. This feeling had grown under the Republican presidents who preceded Roosevelt. Across the country there formed many isolationist groups, which ranged from America First, headed by General Robert E. Wood of Sears, Roebuck, to the more extreme Committee of One Million, headed by Gerald L. K. Smith. There were groups which were angry over the outcome of World War I, groups that feared that entering another war would mean bigger government and more taxes and more power for Roosevelt, groups that thought that war would increase the influence of the military. German-Americans and Italian-Americans also feared the growing resentment of fellow citizens who disliked the dictatorships in Italy and Germany.

Of course, some groups favored intervention in Europe or at least urged that the United States aid Britain and France against Hitler, but the voices of the interventionists were often drowned out by the isolationists.

The fervor for isolationism grew when Senator Gerald Nye launched an investigation of wartime profiteering. He convinced many Americans that the United States had entered World War I purely to line the pockets of arms makers and international bankers and other wealthy people. Some 126,000 Americans had died in the war, and for what? It certainly had not turned out to be the "war to end all wars." Many Americans believed that the war had been fought in vain because of the many compromises made in the Treaty of Versailles and because of the failure of the League of Nations to maintain peace.

Over the next few years, Congress passed neutrality legislation that imposed an embargo on the sale of arms to nations at war, banned loans to all warring nations, and forbade Americans citizens to travel on the ships of nations at war.

Still, Roosevelt viewed the international crisis with alarm. In 1937, as Japan was invading Peking and Nanking in China, he told a crowd in Chicago that Americans should not imagine that they could escape being singed by the international bonfires. "It seems to be unfortunately true that the epidemic of world lawlessness is spreading," he said. "When an epidemic of physical disease starts to

145

spread, the community approves and joins in a quarantine of the patients in order to protect the health of the community against the spread of the disease."[1]

But Roosevelt never pinpointed what the "quarantine" should be. He believed that the democratic nations acting together should be able to check aggressive dictators, but he could not put his concept into words. Furthermore, antiwar feeling still pervaded the United States. Even after Japanese warplanes bombed the U.S. gunboat *Panay* lying at anchor in the Yangtse River in China, the American people and Congress seemed unwilling to strike back. Two crew members died, and eleven were injured. But the Japanese apologized for the incident, and the public was satisfied with the apologies.

In fact, the incident seemed to speed up congressional action on the Ludlow amendment, which called for amending the Constitution so the United States could declare war only when invaded or when a majority of the people voted to go to war in a special referendum.

Roosevelt objected strongly that the referendum idea "would cripple any President in his conduct of our foreign relations."[2] So the measure was finally defeated, but just barely—by a vote of 209–188.

In 1938 the clouds over Europe grew darker and more ominous. In February Hitler invaded Austria and then threatened to take over the Sudetenland of western Czechoslovakia—an area heavily populated by Germans. Prime Minister Neville Chamberlain of Great Britain flew to Munich to negotiate. Although Hitler would probably have backed down if Chamberlain had stood firm, Chamberlain was convinced that if the democracies of Europe opposed Germany, war would break out. So in Munich on September 30, 1938, the Czechs signed away the Sudetenland. "I believe it is peace for our time," Chamberlain told the British when he returned to London to cheers and applause.[3]

Roosevelt's stand at the time seemed ambivalent. Before the agreement at Munich was signed, he had sent messages to England, France, Germany, and Czechoslovakia urging them to keep negotiating. Afterward, he publicly expressed relief at the agreement, but he was also shocked and outraged that England and France would allow Germany to invade Czechoslovakia.

Privately, Roosevelt told others that war was inevitable in the next few years. "Perhaps when it comes the United States will be in a position to pick up the pieces of European civilization and help them to save what remains of the wreck—not a cheerful prospect," he said.[4]

Throughout the year, Roosevelt made an effort to increase the quotas of refugees from Austria and Europe, many of them Jewish, who were fleeing Hitler. He also encouraged other countries to take in the refugees as well. Roosevelt probably could have done more to help the refugees. But there was strong anti-Semitic feeling in the United States during the 1930s that opposed increases in immigration. From the time that Hitler's aggression began until Pearl Harbor, only some 150,000 refugees entered the United States.

Although the appeasement of Hitler may seem shocking to Americans decades later, it bought time for England, France, and the United States to prepare for war. Roosevelt knew that arms production had to be stepped up, and in October 1938 he announced that $300 million would be spent on new American weapons. One of his first goals was to increase the production of military planes in response to the superb air force in Germany. His plan called not only for building up the U.S. air strength but for selling planes to France as well. But he faced political problems.

Although France had not yet declared war on Germany, and therefore was not subject to the arms embargo of the Neutrality Act, isolationists in Congress still opposed the plane sales. But Roosevelt persisted, and by the end of 1939, hundreds of planes had been sent to France.

In the spring of 1939 Roosevelt tried to get Congress to repeal the arms embargo provision of the Neutrality Act, but got nowhere even though war in Europe seemed imminent. In March of that year, Germany overran Czechoslovakia without firing a shot. Soon after, Mussolini invaded Albania. Clearly, Hitler's next target would be Poland. The British and French finally realized that the policies of appeasement had failed. They assured the Polish government that they would stand behind that nation against Hitler.

Meanwhile, Roosevelt sent a message to Hitler and Mussolini asking them not to attack a list of thirty-one nations during the next ten years. In return, he said, the United States would call a disarmament conference. But Hitler and Mussolini only scoffed at and mocked him.

The whole world was shocked in August 1939 when Hitler and Russia's dictator, Stalin, signed a German-Soviet Nonaggression Pact. The agreement included secret provisions that Germany was to seize Lithuania and the Soviets to take Estonia and Latvia. They also plotted to divide Poland between them.

At dawn of September 1, 1939, Roosevelt learned the worst via phone calls from officials in Europe. What had been feared for some time had become reality—German troops were pouring into Poland. The blow had finally been struck that pushed Europe into open conflict. Britain and France declared war on Germany two days later.

In response to these hostilities, Roosevelt was forced to immediately comply with the Neutrality Act and place an embargo on the sale of arms to all the nations involved in the conflict.

Although most Americans favored the cause of the Allies—Britain and France—many still hoped that they could stay out of the war. Strong voices still favored isolationism. On September 15, Charles Lindbergh, the heroic aviator who had made the first solo flight across the Atlantic, made a radio speech warning Americans not to enter the war.

His broadcast led a million Americans to write letters to Congress in favor of his stand.

But Roosevelt knew that the tide had turned in Europe and that new steps were needed. He held talks with Republicans in Congress about repealing the arms embargo. In one of his fireside chats he said he would try to keep the United States out of the war, but he told Americans that he knew that their thoughts would not be neutral about the conflict in Europe. "Even a neutral," he said, "cannot be asked to close his mind or his conscience." [5]

Congress agreed. In early November 1939 the arms embargo was repealed by wide margins in both the Senate and House of Representatives. Both Republicans and Democrats seemed to be uniting in the belief that they must take some stand against Hitler. But still the isolationists had some say—the Allies, Britain and France, had to operate on a "cash and carry" basis; that is, they had to pay cash for the arms they bought and had to carry them away in their own ships. That way the United States could not be dragged into war to protect loans made to buy arms, the isolationists believed. Nor would American ships, loaded with arms for the Allies, be threatened by German submarines.

Early in 1940 the conflict in Europe stalled temporarily. The French army and British navy were on the alert; Hitler was massing his troops on the Dutch and Belgian border. But the situation had turned into what was called the "phony war."

In the United States, Americans were focusing on whether Roosevelt would decide to seek an unprecedented third term in the 1940 elections. Several of his associates wanted to run—Vice President Garner, Secretary of State Cordell Hull, Harry Hopkins, and Postmaster James Farley—but none seemed to have the appeal to voters that Roosevelt had had.

Still, the president seemed ready to retire so that he could follow other interests. Already, he had begun the building of the Roosevelt Library at Hyde Park, where he hoped to organize and edit his public papers. He even signed a contract to write twenty-six articles for *Collier's* magazine. But he refused to say no to the possibility that he might run again. Polls indicated that most Americans thought he could win a third term.

Then, in the spring of 1940, the Germans invaded Norway and Denmark, and after that the Netherlands and Belgium. Soon the Nazis were moving toward Paris. England's prime minister, Winston Churchill, tried to bolster the French forces and to induce them to fight on. The desperate French appealed to Roosevelt to intervene before they sought peace from Hitler. Roosevelt believed he could not help them, even though he wrote to French leaders saying that he was doing everything he could to send supplies to the Allies in Europe.

Alarmed by the crisis and fearing that the British would be the next to crumble, Roosevelt scraped together what leftover World War I equipment he could find in May 1940 to rush it off to Britain. Although the rifles and machine guns he sent were almost obsolete, he took the action privately at first. Later, it was announced publicly.

Also in May, Roosevelt appeared before Congress to ask for the building of 50,000 new airplanes and a defense appropriation of $900 million. At the time American factories were only beginning to gear up for production of war materials.

The Army also numbered only about a half million men, and it lacked up-to-date and sufficient weapons. But because the isolationist fervor remained strong, Roosevelt hesitated to ask Congress to seek a military draft.

In late June 1940 the French capitulated to Hitler. France was split in two, with one section governed by the Germans. The other half, with its seat of power at the city of Vichy, was put under the control of Nazi-approved French officials. They were led by a World War I hero, Henri-Philippe Pétain, who had sued Hitler for peace.

To promote national unity and avoid criticism of his policies, Roosevelt organized new defense agencies and appointed two Republicans to his cabinet: Henry Stimson as secretary of war and Frank Knox as secretary of the navy. In October 1940 Congress voted to spend $17 billion on preparations for war. Defense agreements were also worked out with Latin American nations.

But both Republicans and Democrats tried to avoid debating the question of whether the United States should become involved in the war as they prepared for the 1940 elections. The problem was that the nation was still torn between isolationists and the interventionists or internationalists, who wanted to support the European democracies or declare war on Germany. Among the interventionist groups were the Committee to Defend America by Aiding the Allies and the Century Group.

As the threat of war grew, the Republicans dropped the candidate they had originally favored, Senator Robert Taft of Ohio, known for his isolationist views. Instead they chose a dark-horse candidate with more-moderate ideas on international issues, Wendell Willkie, a former Democrat who had became a strong critic of the New Deal. Willkie was president of the Commonwealth and Southern Utility Company, an organization that had led a fight against the Tennessee Valley Authority. At the GOP convention in Philadelphia, delegates were flooded with telegrams supporting Willkie, and young Willkie backers sitting in the galleries relentlessly shouted, "We want Willkie!" On the sixth ballot their candidate was nominated.

It seemed unlikely to most Democrats that anyone but Roosevelt could defeat the popular and attractive Willkie. Although by the time of the convention Roosevelt had decided to run again, he refused to say so publicly right up until the end and insisted that the delegates were free to vote as they pleased. He even declined to attend the convention, held in Chicago in July. Like the Republicans, the Democrats were also troubled about what stand to take on the European war. "We will not send our armed forces to fight in lands across the sea," they finally wrote into their platform, but Roosevelt phoned and persuaded the platform committee to add the words "except in case of attack." [6]

On the evening of July 16 the convention chairman, Alben Barkley, read a message to the delegates in which Roosevelt said he had no wish to remain as president or in any public office after January 1941. But the delegates held a tumultuous demonstration in which they shouted loud and long: "We want Roosevelt!"

The next day Roosevelt was nominated on the first ballot with 946 votes. His four opponents, Farley, Garner, Hull, and Senator Millard Tydings of Maryland, received only a total of 147. Afterward, Henry Wallace, the secretary of agriculture, was chosen as Roosevelt's running mate. He was not a popular choice, but he was the man that Roosevelt wanted. James Farley, who had become increasingly disillusioned with Roosevelt, was particularly upset at the outcome of the convention and afterward resigned his job as postmaster general.

Willkie immediately hit the campaign trail, while Roosevelt stayed in Washington. The president enjoyed playing the role of the chief executive too busy with affairs of state to spend time answering the charges of his opponent. But even though Willkie often made clumsy and silly blunders in his speeches, he was a strong campaigner and the first opponent who seemed to have a chance against Roosevelt. In fifty-one days of the campaign he traveled 19,000 miles and gave 500 speeches in thirty states. What was more, the powerful labor leader John L. Lewis, who had had a falling-out with Roosevelt, had urged members of the CIO to vote for Willkie.

In September a bill was introduced in Congress calling for the first peacetime draft in American history. Isolationists fought hard against it, but the Selective Service

152

Act was adopted, calling for an army of 1.4 million men to be raised by a lottery draft.

Although Willkie had favored the draft, he began to label Roosevelt as a warmonger, using the catchphrase "A vote for Roosevelt is a vote for war." He even attacked a deal that Roosevelt had made to send a number of old destroyers to Great Britain in return for bases in Newfoundland and the West Indies.

Finally, under pressure from his advisers, Roosevelt launched a campaign just before the election to fight back. Because of Willkie's attacks he felt he had to promise the voters: "I have said this before, but I shall say it again and again and again: 'Your boys are not going to be sent into foreign wars.' "[7] It was a statement he later regretted deeply.

On Election Day Roosevelt returned as usual to Hyde Park to vote and await the returns. This time he was concerned about the outcome of the election, despite political polls that seemed encouraging. He sat alone in the mansion's dining room that night with tally sheets of votes in front of him.

He need not have worried. The final vote was 27,244,160 for Roosevelt to 22,305,198 for Willkie. Willkie won only 82 electoral votes, less than a quarter of Roosevelt's 449. Once the results were known, Willkie conceded gracefully and later supported the president's efforts to provide aid to Great Britain.

After the election Roosevelt came up with a new way to help the opponents of the Axis powers (Germany, Italy, and Japan). It was the Lend-Lease plan, designed to get around the isolationists who insisted that Roosevelt could not send arms or ships to Britain without the British paying for them. Although the British had paid before, it was unlikely that they could keep doing so. So in late 1940 Roosevelt proposed "leasing" several hundred merchant ships to the British, whose shipping industry had been crippled by the Germans. It was a subterfuge, of course. Even the isolationists in Congress pointed out that it was unlikely that after the war the United States would want the ships back.

But Roosevelt explained at a press conference that if his neighbor's home were on fire he would let him use his garden hose to put the fire out and would certainly not ask him to pay for the hose. "I don't want $15," he said, "I want my garden hose back after the fire is over." [8]

A few weeks later, in one of his fireside chats, Roosevelt told Americans that they must do all they could to support the opponents of the Axis powers even though the United States was trying to avoid war. "We must be the great arsenal of democracy," he said. [9]

Finally, on March 11, after a bitter battle in the Congress, the Lend-Lease bill was signed into law. Roosevelt quickly sent lists of available weapons to Britain and Greece and asked Congress for $7 billion to begin the new program. Roosevelt chose Hopkins to run the Lend-Lease program and sent him to England to confer with Prime Minister Churchill.

In Europe in early 1941 there were more threats that Hitler was on the move again. He pressured Franco to allow him to take over Gibraltar and then to move from there into Africa, but Franco refused. Hitler also seemed ready to aid the Italians who were fighting in Libya. Or would he invade the Balkans?

In the spring the Germans swept quickly into Yugoslavia and Greece and then took over the island of Crete. The British failed to hold them off; they were desperate for tanks, guns, and other supplies. In North Africa Hitler's general Erwin Rommel was also pushing forward.

For some time Hitler had prevented his navy from attacking American shipping. He feared the power of the United States and hoped to avoid involving Americans in the war too soon. But early in June a German submarine sank an American freighter headed for South Africa as it sailed through the South Atlantic. All the passengers and crew were saved. Although public reaction to the incident was mild, Roosevelt froze the assets of Germany and its ally Italy and ordered German consulates to close—but he did not break off diplomatic relations with Germany.

On June 22, 1941, a crucial turning point was reached. Hitler launched Operation Barbarossa and invaded his one-time ally, Russia, in a surprise attack. Many Americans, who liked the Soviets no better than they liked the Germans, were delighted. Perhaps the two dictatorships would destroy each other.

Despite their distaste for the Soviet Union and its dictator, Joseph Stalin, both British prime minister Winston Churchill and Roosevelt agreed that the Soviet Union must receive aid. If the Soviets could stand fast and keep Hitler's troops bogged down, America might never have to enter the war. Roosevelt sent Hopkins to Russia to meet with Stalin, who asked for $2 billion in arms and supplies.

In August 1941 Churchill and his aides sailed on a British battleship into Placentia Bay, off Newfoundland in Canada. On this ship, for the first time, Roosevelt met face-to-face with Churchill, who had become prime minister in 1940. Almost alone among British leaders, Churchill had raised the alarm against Hitler from 1933 to 1939 and had urged his nation to rearm. It wasn't until Poland was invaded that the British began to listen to his pleas. Now his vigorous leadership and eloquence were bolstering the British as England endured continual bombing by Hitler's air force.

Churchill hoped to get Roosevelt to occupy the Azores, off Portugal, or to attack North Africa, but Roosevelt made no promises. Instead the two made a joint declaration known as the Atlantic Charter. They declared that their countries were not seeking new territory and did not want territorial changes that would violate the wishes of the people concerned. They respected the right of all peoples to choose the form of government under which they wanted to live.

155

They also advocated a permanent peace once the Nazis were destroyed. After this meeting the United States seemed to move ever closer toward war with the Germans in the Atlantic.

More and more, Roosevelt's focus was turning from the domestic problems of his nation to questions that involved the fate of the entire world. When the conflict and upheaval were over, Roosevelt believed, the world could be a very different place based on the course that he and other world leaders set.

These months of international turmoil were also a time of personal crisis for Roosevelt. In the spring of 1941 Roosevelt's faithful secretary, Missy LeHand, suffered a stroke that left her partly paralyzed. She was never able to return to work for him again.

Then, in early September 1941, Roosevelt's mother, Sara, died after a long illness. One of her last wishes was that after her death her room at Hyde Park would be arranged the way it had been at the time her son was born. She knew that at some time or another the Hyde Park mansion would become a national museum to honor her son, already acknowledged as one of America's most influential presidents.

Her death was a great sorrow to Roosevelt even though, as Eleanor said, "He had grown away from her in some ways and . . . in later years they had often not been in sympathy about policies on public affairs." [10] But despite the differences of mother and son, she had always been fiercely loyal to him and had supported him financially as well as emotionally.

15

"A date which will live in infamy"

For several days before December 7, 1941, there had been signs that the Japanese might attack at any time somewhere in the Pacific. Japanese troop ships had been seen moving south. Roosevelt was warned that key Japanese embassies had been ordered to destroy their code books. Roosevelt and his advisers feared and expected an attack on American bases in the Philippines or somewhere else in the Pacific.

Still Roosevelt hoped to avoid war. On the evening of December 6 he sent a final appeal for peace to Japan's emperor Hirohito; the reply was definitely negative. When Roosevelt told Harry Hopkins that he expected war, Hopkins said it was too bad the United States could not strike the first blow. "No we can't do that," Roosevelt said. "We are a democracy and a peaceful people."[1]

Since then, some critics of Roosevelt have charged that he knew what was coming and had allowed the Navy to suffer a severe blow so that he could push the United States into war. But Roosevelt loved the Navy and had close ties to many of its officers. Two of his sons were in the Navy, and one was a Marine. He had feared that an attack was coming, but his main goal was to prevent war.

The next afternoon as Roosevelt ate lunch with Hopkins, a message was wired to him from the commander in chief of the Pacific fleet—the Japanese had attacked Pearl Harbor, near Honolulu, Hawaii, and done severe damage. Partly due to carelessness, American commanders in Hawaii had been caught by surprise.

Eight battleships, three light cruisers, three destroyers, and four other vessels were sunk or badly damaged. One hundred sixty-seven airplanes were destroyed, and another 128 damaged. More than 2,400 Americans were killed; another 1,178 were wounded. The U.S. Navy had suffered a crushing blow.

War had arrived. As Roosevelt received fresh details about the devastation, he grew more severe, more serious, but also very calm. "I thought that in spite of his anxiety Franklin was in a way more serene than he had appeared in a long time," Eleanor said. "I think it was steadying to know finally that the die was cast. One could no longer do anything but face the fact that this country was in a war."[2]

As the day wore on, a crowd of a thousand people thronged Pennsylvania Avenue to watch as cars full of officials drove through the White House gates. Even after darkness fell, hundreds still pressed against the iron fence of the White House. Americans were stunned and somewhat fearful but also outraged.

After sleeping only five hours, Roosevelt rose early to get to work in the Oval Office. Not only had the Japanese attacked in Hawaii, he was told, they had also attacked Hong Kong, Guam, the Philippines, Wake Island, and Midway Island.

At about noon a car drove him with Eleanor and son James to the Capitol. The mood along Pennsylvania Avenue was solemn. The sparse crowds on the street knew what was coming. Inside the chamber of the House of Representatives, every seat was filled by representatives

158

and senators. The doorkeeper called out, "Mister Speaker, the President of the United States," and Roosevelt moved slowly down the aisle to the speaker's podium as he leaned on the arm of his son. There were several rounds of applause and then silence.

Grasping the podium, Roosevelt spoke his immortal words: "Yesterday, December 7, 1941—a date which will live in infamy—the United States of America was suddenly and deliberately attacked by naval and air forces of the Empire of Japan.

" . . . Hostilities exist. There is no blinking at the fact that our people, our territory, and our interests are in grave danger.

"With confidence in our armed forces, with the unbounding determination of our people—we will gain the inevitable triumph—so help us God." [3]

Congress followed by declaring war on Japan. Shortly after, the Germans declared war on the United States, and the United States responded by entering the war against Germany and Italy.

A grim Christmas followed as the Japanese burned a trail through the South Pacific. Winston Churchill flew into Washington for the holidays to confer with Roosevelt and the president's growing staff of generals and admirals about what to do next. The two leaders even stood side by side on the White House portico for the traditional lighting of the presidential Christmas tree.

Where would the United States concentrate its major war effort, Churchill wondered, in fighting the Japanese in the Pacific or in freeing Europe from Hitler's domination? Roosevelt assured Churchill that Europe was his main concern. For starters, Churchill wanted the United States to move troops into North Africa, but Roosevelt was hesitant to do so. Soviet dictator Joseph Stalin, meanwhile, pressured Roosevelt to begin a second front in Europe to take pressure off the Russian troops who were battling the Germans.

159

Roosevelt wasn't as interested in mapping military strategy as he was in stating clearly what the associated countries, or United Nations, as the Allies decided to call themselves, aimed to do. An agreement was finally signed on January 1, 1942, calling for the "United Nations," including the United States, Great Britain, and their many allies, to fight the Axis countries. Each member nation promised not to make a separate peace with the enemies. Over the next few weeks, Roosevelt obtained the consent of twenty-six countries to the pact as he increasingly moved to take charge of the war effort worldwide. The United States had only just entered the war, but Roosevelt already seemed the chief leader of the Allies.

As the new year began, much of Roosevelt's energy went into increasing production of materials and weapons for the war. New agencies had to be created to coordinate which factories would get steel and coal and wood and oil, to decide which branch of the service would get what it wanted. Roosevelt set up the War Production Board to make these decisions. Another federal agency, the Office of Price Administration, had been organized in early 1941 to hold the line on prices and to ration scarce materials.

A key problem was finding enough rubber to meet wartime needs. Synthetic rubber was not being produced fast enough, and the sources of natural rubber were in the hands of the Japanese. Roosevelt appealed over the radio to get Americans to turn in old tires, garden hoses, bathing caps, gloves made of rubber to their local gas stations. Gasoline was also in short supply because of German attacks on oil tankers. Eventually, although reluctantly, Roosevelt agreed to rationing both gas and rubber.

Although Roosevelt's attitude toward all these problems was that his staff should come up with answers themselves so that he could concentrate on diplomacy and war strategy, many times he had to resolve disputes and conflicts.

Life in the White House took on a wartime flavor.

160

Tourists could no longer visit the first-floor rooms. Anti-aircraft guns were installed on the White House roof and large platoons of soldiers guarded the gates.

The war dominated the nation's thoughts and emotions. Americans bought war bonds in record numbers and tried to make do with less of everything as factories shifted their production from consumer goods to military supplies. Movies, plays, and songs with a wartime theme were wildly popular.

The war brought tremendous changes in the lives of workers as millions of people, mostly men, went off to military service. Women took over driving trucks and running heavy machinery; women workers increased by almost 2 million in the year after Pearl Harbor. Blacks and other minority groups also found increased chances for getting better jobs as the demand for labor grew. Several months before the war, Roosevelt had signed an executive order requiring defense industries to hire workers without regard for race, creed, color, or national origin. All defense contracts included this provision, and a Committee on Fair Employment Practices was set up, although it had very little police power.

Early in 1942 the news from the Pacific was dismal. Perhaps the heaviest blow was the fall of the Philippines to the Japanese in March. The United States could do little to save that country, but the fight went on until U.S. general Douglas MacArthur fled to Australia. Soon the Japanese had also overpowered Singapore and Borneo and had overrun an area stretching from Sumatra through Java to New Guinea and the Solomon Islands. India and Australia seemed to be next on the list of conquests.

As they moved through the Pacific, the Japanese issued a call to fellow Asians to shake off the bonds of white colonial governments. Some feared that India might rebel against its British colonial government and ally itself with Japan. As a way of preventing such a rebellion, Roosevelt tried to get Britain to promise independence for India once

161

the war was over—in line with the principles that he and Churchill had agreed to in the Atlantic Charter. But Churchill was opposed and offered only dominion status to India after the war. Roosevelt went along with Churchill's decision, and in fact India did not try to shake off British rule during the war.

At first, after the guns began to fire, Roosevelt's popularity had grown, but then polls showed that Americans were losing confidence in him. To bolster public opinion he believed he had to remind Americans that tough times lay ahead. It was a different kind of war, he told the nation, in a Washington's Birthday speech. "It is warfare in terms of every continent, every island, every sea, every air lane in the world."[4]

Early in 1942 Roosevelt agreed to what was later regarded as one of the most shameful actions of his presidency. In California, racism and intolerance grew as residents read about the march of the Japanese through the Pacific. There were false reports of flashing lights offshore in the Pacific Ocean—supposedly signals to Japanese-American spies. There was unreasonable fear that many Japanese-Americans would be sympathetic to an invasion by Japan on the West Coast.

Many California state officials pressured the White House to act. In response, key advisers sought Roosevelt's opinion. He told them to do what they thought necessary. A few days later he signed an evacuation order that removed more than 100,000 Japanese-Americans from their homes on the West Coast and interned them in concentration camps in isolated inland areas. Congress later endorsed the plan, and there was little public outcry from the press. Those of German and Italian descent presented the same alleged threat to their fellow Americans, but no action was taken against them.

In the spring of 1942 there were hopeful signs about the progress of the war. The Japanese navy launched an assault on the United States Fleet at Midway Island in the

South Pacific. The Americans were prepared and heavily armed and managed to destroy four Japanese aircraft carriers, a heavy cruiser, and 330 planes. The Americans lost one carrier and 150 planes. A long battle still lay ahead in the South Pacific, but if the Japanese had captured Midway, they could easily have moved on to the Hawaiian Islands. Instead, they had to fall back and take a defensive position in the territory they had already claimed.

Meanwhile, Stalin continued to push his demands for the Americans and British to launch an attack across the English Channel. Secretary of War Henry Stimson and generals George Marshall and Dwight Eisenhower agreed with this concept and prepared a plan to attack in April 1943. At first, Roosevelt seemed to favor this date for an invasion, but later, when Soviet foreign minister Vyacheslav Molotov visited the United States, Roosevelt went further and promised to attack in the fall of 1942. Molotov had convinced him that without military relief Russia might fall to the Germans. In fact, the Russians later hinted at the possibility that they might have to make a separate peace with Germany.

Marshall was upset that Roosevelt had moved up the date. Then Churchill began throwing up roadblocks. The Allies were not ready for a cross-channel offensive so soon; too many heavily armed Germans were stationed in France. The British pushed for an assault on North Africa, where they believed victory would be easier to grasp.

In June, while Churchill visited Roosevelt again, word came that Tobruk, a key city in North Africa, had fallen to the Nazis. Twenty-five thousand Allied soldiers had been taken prisoner. The British were firm; they needed American tanks and men in North Africa. Roosevelt agreed to postpone the second front in Europe.

At first, Stalin seemed furious; the Germans had taken the Crimea, were moving on Stalingrad, and were about to swarm into Soviet oil fields near the Black Sea. But later, he seemed to accept the change of plans. It's hard to know

163

what the cold-blooded and brutal Stalin was actually thinking, but for many Soviets the delay in the second front was a severe blow. It meant that hundreds of thousands of Russians starved to death or were killed by the Germans. Soviet animosity over the delay in the second front lasted for many years after World War II.

Meanwhile, in the Atlantic the German U-boats, or submarines, took a heavy toll on American shipping. Not only did America need many new naval vessels, it also needed many new cargo ships so that it could continue to speed supplies to its European allies.

By the spring of 1942 America's shipyards had responded to Roosevelt's calls for a massive increase in production and were building the cargo vessels known as the Liberty ships in only sixty or seventy days each.

After years of trying to promote higher prices, Roosevelt found after Pearl Harbor that the war was creating runaway inflation, particularly in the cost of food. In response, workers demanded hefty wage increases. Roosevelt created a new National War Labor Board to help settle strikes and labor disputes and to set wages. A Stabilization Act was passed in October 1942 which worked to stabilize food prices and to impose rent control. An Office of Economic Stabilization was created, and Roosevelt appointed a former senator and key aide, James Byrnes, as its director to work on holding down prices, profits, and wages.

Roosevelt also pushed for increasing taxes as a way of controlling inflation and to keep companies from making outrageous profits from wartime production.

At times Roosevelt seemed to handle these problems on a piecemeal basis. He seemed to do little long-range planning or thinking ahead, but when a crisis hit, he swung into action with some new agency or program.

During the early years of the war, Roosevelt endorsed secret plans for American scientists to work on a powerful new weapon, the atom bomb. It was feared that German scientists, who had already done much of the research on

164

splitting the atom, might be close to unlocking the secrets of this bomb. No one knew how long it might take to develop an atomic bomb in the United States or what its impact might be on the war, but by the end of 1942 hundreds of scientists and workers from all over the world were brought to Los Alamos, New Mexico, to work secretly on this weapon.

In November 1942, Allied forces, commanded by U.S. general Dwight Eisenhower, began the invasion of northwest Africa, an area still controlled by the Vichy government of France. The operation, with the code name Torch, was the invasion that Winston Churchill had wanted for so long. Roosevelt's government had remained in touch with the Vichy officials and had hoped that the French forces could be persuaded to lay down their arms without fighting. Marshal Pétain ordered the French soldiers to battle on, but another Vichy official, Admiral Jean-François Darlan, agreed to a cease-fire. After the Allies took control, they put Darlan in charge of French North Africa.

Roars of protest over this deal came from liberals, from the press, and from the Free French forces outside of France. How could Roosevelt and his government ally themselves with a Nazi-collaborator like Darlan? Why didn't Roosevelt appoint General Charles de Gaulle, the Free French leader whose popularity was growing worldwide? Darlan's appointment also raised questions in the minds of Soviet leaders about how strong a stand Roosevelt would make against Hitler.

Roosevelt was unhappy with the situation. At a press conference he admitted, "I thoroughly understand and approve the feeling that . . . no permanent arrangement should be made with Admiral Darlan."[5] But he felt that a quick end to the warfare in North Africa was vital. Every soldier who died fighting the Vichy French meant one less man to face the Germans, who still controlled much of North Africa.

Just before Christmas 1942 Darlan was assassinated,

however, and another French leader, General Henri Giraud, who was more respectable in the eyes of the Allies, took control.

But it took until May 1943 for British and American forces to drive the Germans and Italians out of Africa. More than 70,000 Allied soldiers were killed and wounded in the effort.

In January 1943 Roosevelt and Churchill met in Casablanca, Morocco, to discuss the war effort. It was the first of a series of conferences that had momentous effects on the war and also on the future of the world after the war. Roosevelt had hoped that Stalin might also come to Casablanca, but he was unable to do so.

Roosevelt broke tradition with his trip to Casablanca. It was the first time that an American president had ever visited a war zone. And not only that, Roosevelt flew there.

At these sessions with world leaders, Roosevelt made full use of the charm and charisma that served him well politically in his own country. Sometimes he seemed hesitant to make firm decisions about policies and procedures and about plans for peace. Often he agreed verbally to some matters without seeming to fully realize what he had said. Some have speculated that his hesitancy partly stemmed from his fears that he might end up like President Woodrow Wilson, fighting to the death to defend the unworkable Treaty of Versailles after World War I. But for the most part, he was in charge of these conferences and his decisions were the ones that counted most.

During ten days of discussion, Churchill argued for the Allies to move up from North Africa to a landing on the island of Sicily off Italy. The cross-channel attack into France, eventually code-named Overlord, was going to have to wait until 1944 because so many soldiers had been committed to the fighting in Africa. Although U.S. general George Marshall argued against launching the operation in Sicily, the British generals persuaded Roosevelt to go ahead.

At Casablanca, Roosevelt also met for the first time

with de Gaulle, who had come to the session only very reluctantly. Roosevelt was suspicious of de Gaulle and his quest for power, and de Gaulle did not like the American president either. He particularly resisted Roosevelt's efforts to get him to cooperate with Henri Giraud. "Roosevelt showed himself eager to reach a meeting of minds, using charm rather than reason to convince me, but attached once and for all to the decisions he had made," de Gaulle later wrote.[6]

De Gaulle wanted France freed as soon as possible and quickly restored as a world power. Roosevelt believed that it would take some time before France could be liberated and also wanted the French to give up their colonies after the war.

However, Roosevelt did persuade de Gaulle and Giraud to sign a document setting up ties between them and got them to shake hands for photographers.

At a press conference for war correspondents at the end of the session, Roosevelt made a startling announcement, one completely unexpected by Churchill. "The elimination of German, Japanese and Italian war power means the unconditional surrender by Germany, Italy or Japan," he told the press. That did not mean that those countries would be totally destroyed, he went on, but it did mean "the destruction of the philosophies in those countries which are based on conquest and the subjugation of other people."[7] Observers thought that Churchill seemed surprised at how far Roosevelt had gone, but he agreed with Roosevelt in his own statement.

Later Roosevelt contended that the call for an unconditional surrender had simply "popped into my mind,"[8] but the truth was that he and his advisers had been discussing the concept for some time. The only surprise was that he announced it publicly without discussing it first with other Allied leaders.

Many political writers have since contended that this announcement toughened the resolve of German soldiers

167

and gave Hitler a propaganda weapon to use against the Allies. One German general later wrote: "The soldiers . . . were convinced from now on that our enemies had decided on the utter destruction of Germany, that they were no longer fighting . . . against Hitler and so-called Nazis, but against their efficient, and therefore dangerous, rivals for the trade of the world."[9]

On July 10, 1943, the British and Americans landed in Sicily. The invasion cost 20,000 Allied dead and wounded, but the Sicilians greeted the invaders as liberators. Twelve thousand Germans were killed or captured, but another 60,000 German soldiers fled the island. Once Sicily fell, Mussolini was deposed. Then, on September 9, American and British forces landed at Salerno, near Naples in Italy. The Italian government surrendered quickly, but Allied soldiers had to fight for some time against German divisions in Italy.

Roosevelt and Churchill met together twice more in 1943—once in Quebec in August in a meeting code-named Quadrant, and once in Cairo in November in a meeting they named Sextant. The Quebec meeting focused on more debate over strategy for the war. Churchill pressed Roosevelt to use the invasion of Italy to move up into the Balkan countries in southern Europe to keep the Soviet Union from takeovers there. But Roosevelt wanted Overlord, the invasion of France, to take place on May 1, 1944.

The two also agreed that their two countries would do joint research on atomic energy but would not share their knowledge with the Soviet Union.

At the Sextant conference, China was the main concern. Roosevelt wanted to enhance China's prestige and make that country a major force after the war. He believed that four great powers, the United States, Britain, the Soviet Union, and China, could cooperate after the war in maintaining world peace and security, although China was far from stable politically at the time. He also thought that the Chinese could aid the United States against Japan.

168

Roosevelt and Churchill discussed a military assault in the Far East to help China, but the plans never went ahead. They did commit themselves to restoring to China the lands she had lost to Japan during the war.

But the major conference of 1943 was yet to come. In Tehran, Iran, Roosevelt, who was emerging as the most powerful leader in the world, would finally meet his strongest rival, the dictator of the Soviet Union, Joseph Stalin.

16

"Dr. Win-the-War"

After their meeting in Cairo, Roosevelt and Churchill flew on to Tehran for their Big Three meeting with Joseph Stalin. Roosevelt had protested that Teheran was too far away for the meeting, but Stalin had insisted that the other leaders meet him in Iran.

Roosevelt had planned to stay at the American Legation, but shortly after he arrived he was told of an alleged assassination plot brewing against the three leaders. At Stalin's invitation he moved into the more secure Russian embassy, where the discussions were held. There the leaders and their aides gathered for their meetings around a 10-foot-wide round oak table specially built for the occasion.

From the beginning the always-confident Roosevelt believed that he could control the balky and erratic Stalin through the charm of his personality. He expected that during the meetings he would establish a strong relationship with Stalin that could help in building a firm peace once the war ended. But not everyone at the meeting was sure that Stalin could be trusted. Roosevelt, so successful in persuading the American Congress and voters to do his bidding, faced a much stiffer task in the case of Joseph Stalin.

According to a British interpreter at the session, Roosevelt "beamed on all around the table and looked very much like the kind, rich uncle paying a visit to his poorer relations. . . . He spoke firmly, as if sure of his ground, but at the same time appeared ready to listen to the promptings of his advisers who sat alongside."[1]

Roosevelt seemed thoroughly in command of the meetings, but still the British were apprehensive of what the American president was thinking. They believed that Roosevelt did not thoroughly understand the kind of person Stalin was. They were particularly upset when Roosevelt seemed to take sides with Stalin against Churchill and began pushing the British to give up the domination of their colonial empire.

Stalin also continued to argue for a cross-channel attack on the Germans and opposed the suggestion that the Allied forces push from Italy up into the Balkan countries. If the Allies had gone into the Balkans, it might have thwarted Stalin's own plans for that area—plans of which Roosevelt and Churchill were largely unaware. Meanwhile, Stalin promised Roosevelt that once the Germans were defeated, the Soviet forces would join the Americans in fighting Japan in the Pacific. Churchill wanted to postpone Overlord (the cross-channel attack) again, but in the end he agreed that it should take place during May 1944.

Roosevelt also proposed to Stalin that, after the war, peacekeeping in the world be controlled by what he called "four policemen"—the Soviet Union, the United States, Great Britain, and China. There would also be a worldwide United Nations which would discuss nonmilitary matters. But Stalin favored having regional councils in Europe and the Far East instead and objected that it was unlikely China would be a world power after the war ended.

One topic discussed at Tehran would later cause great controversy. For some time Roosevelt had toyed with various ideas about what the map of Europe should look like after the war, and during the conference he and Stalin talked about the postwar boundaries of the Balkan countries and of Poland and Germany. Only a short time before, Roosevelt had helped to draw up the idealistic Atlantic Charter, which argued that individual nations should determine their own fate. How could he then go to Tehran, many people later asked, and callously join Stalin in redrawing the geography of Eastern Europe?

At first, Roosevelt told Stalin that he did not wish to alienate the 6 million or 7 million Polish-American voters in the 1944 elections by harming Poland in some way. The Poles should determine their own fate and boundaries. Therefore, he said, he would not discuss Poland's future at the Tehran conference. But later, Roosevelt went on to do just that and agreed verbally with Stalin that the Soviet Union could take over some of Poland's eastern territory. To make up for this loss of territory, the two agreed, Poland could then take over some of Germany on its western border. Roosevelt also joked that he personally would not be ready to wage war with the Soviet Union if Russia reoccupied the tiny nations of Latvia, Estonia, and Lithuania, but that Americans would want these areas to determine their own fate. Stalin was disgruntled and told Roosevelt that "some propaganda work should be done" to persuade American voters that these Baltic nations belonged inside the Soviet Union.[2]

Roosevelt left the conference pleased, partly because a final agreement said that the three leaders would fight to eliminate tyranny and oppression throughout the world. He was also pleased that Churchill had finally agreed to a cross-channel attack. But his aides were not so sure that the conference had succeeded. One wrote a memo indicating that it was clear that the Soviet Union planned on becoming the most important power in postwar Europe. "The rest of Europe would be reduced to military and political impotence," this aide later wrote.[3]

After that, the Roosevelts spent a happy Christmas with a flock of their children and grandchildren at Hyde Park. The president was still buoyed up with feelings of success over the Tehran meeting. But by the time the holidays had ended, he had come down with a bad case of the flu that signaled the start of a series of illnesses that troubled him for the next few months.

In Washington his own political problems were growing. He found the coalition of Old Guard Republicans and conservative Democrats stronger than ever in Congress and throwing up opposition to his domestic legislation. Some Southern Democrats were even threatening to form a third political party. Still, everyone believed that Roosevelt would probably run again in 1944. Eleanor, who had not wanted him to seek a third term, felt that he should serve a fourth time in spite of his failing health: "If he can accomplish what he set out to do, and then dies, it will have been worth it. I agree with him."[4]

Early in 1944, Roosevelt battled Congress on his proposals for tax increases and price-fixing measures to handle inflation. Prices had risen 25 percent over what they had been in 1941. There was a growing black market for rationed household items. Roosevelt pleaded with Congress for action. In the end Congress passed a tax bill with only $2 billion in increases, not the $10.5 billion that Roosevelt wanted. The Senate majority leader, Alben Barkley, even refused to back Roosevelt when the president vetoed the tax bill, and Congress ended up overriding his veto.

Roosevelt also faced crises with labor unions and had to order the army to step in to run the railroads because of a train workers' strike.

Because the nation was becoming more conservative, Roosevelt began to modify his liberal stands slightly. He told the press that it might be time to retire the term "New Deal." "The remedies that old Dr. New Deal used were for internal trouble. But at the present time, obviously the principal emphasis, the overwhelming first emphasis should be on winning the war," he said. It was time to call in "Dr. Win-the-War."[5]

That statement upset Eleanor and several of Roosevelt's more liberal advisers. But in early January 1944, when he gave his State of the Union address to Congress, he was more militant again, calling for "a second Bill of Rights under which a new basis of security and prosperity can be established for all—regardless of station or race or creed."[6] He also called for the right of every family to have a decent home, adequate medical care, and freedom from fears about old age and unemployment, and to have a good education.

As time went on, Roosevelt's health grew worse and worse. He had stomach ailments and trouble with his sinuses. His face grew gray and tired. He developed headaches and suffered from chronic fatigue. He found food tasteless and began to lose weight. For years he had prided himself on his ability to take care of himself in spite of his disabilities. But toward the end of the war, he became more dependent on others to lift him from wheelchair to office chair. He delegated more of his power to those who worked for him. He was less inclined to visit the military map room of the White House where the progress of forces around the world were outlined.

During this time in the White House, Roosevelt renewed his visits with Lucy Mercer Rutherfurd, who had been widowed, the woman with whom he had had a romance so many years before. Eleanor had made him promise never to see her again, but he had invited Lucy to his inaugurations and visited with her from time to time. During 1944 he occasionally had dinner or tea with her, usually with other friends present.

Because Roosevelt's health kept deteriorating, his physician, Admiral Ross McIntire, the surgeon general of the navy, eventually sent him to Bethesda Naval Hospital for a complete physical. There another doctor found that Roosevelt had hypertension, or high blood pressure, and

174

some degree of heart failure. But McIntire forbade discussion of the case with the Roosevelt family or Roosevelt himself and also vetoed a recommendation that Roosevelt have complete bed rest for several weeks. But when Roosevelt grew even worse, he did agree to changes in the president's lifestyle. Roosevelt was to work in bed in the morning and go to his office only in the afternoon. His diet was changed to one low in fat and salt-free. He had to cut down on his smoking. He also began taking the heart drug digitalis.

Meanwhile, McIntire disclosed nothing about Roosevelt's health to the outside world—nothing that could have hindered Roosevelt's plans to run for a fourth term in 1944. When rumors about Roosevelt's well-being persisted, Admiral McIntire issued bulletins saying that the president was in fine health.

Although the war continued in the Pacific and Europe, clearly events had swung in favor of the Allies. The feeling grew that the war might end soon. On Memorial Day 1944 it was announced that representatives of the United States, Great Britain, the Soviet Union, and China would begin meeting in August in Washington, D.C. The end result of this conference was the drafting of the charter for the United Nations, the worldwide peacekeeping agency that Roosevelt had dreamed of organizing.

As June arrived, the Allied forces were finally ready for D-Day, Operation Overlord, the long-awaited, long-discussed landing in France. The great attack was aimed at 60 miles of beaches in Normandy. A million and a half Americans, another million British and Canadians, and thousands of Norwegian, Danish, French, Belgian, Czech, and Polish soldiers participated, many of them pouring ashore in 4,000 vessels.

Throughout the weekend Roosevelt waited tensely for word of the landing, which had to be slightly delayed due to bad weather. Finally, at four o'clock on Tuesday morning, June 6, he received word that the long-awaited attack on the Germans had been launched the day before. Roosevelt was buoyant and happy when he met with reporters that day. That evening he led the nation in a solemn prayer for the soldiers. "Lead them straight and true; give strength to their arms, stoutness to their hearts; steadfastness in their faith. They will need Thy blessings. Their road will be long and hard." [7]

By July the Allies had taken the beaches of Normandy and the port of Cherbourg, but then the fighting bogged down. From the beginning of the battle for Normandy on June 6 to the end on August 19, the Allied forces lost a total of 170,000 in dead and wounded—68,000 British and Canadian and 102,000 Americans. For the Germans the toll was far worse—between 250,000 and 300,000 men killed or captured. By mid-August the German army was fleeing through the north of France away from the pursuing Allies.

As portions of France were liberated, General Dwight Eisenhower, the supreme commander of the invasion, tried to persuade Roosevelt that he must improve his relations with de Gaulle because most of the French viewed de Gaulle as their leader. Eventually, Roosevelt invited de Gaulle to Washington, and by the fall the French general and his forces had received official recognition as the provisional government of France.

As the Democratic Convention approached in mid-July 1944, there was little doubt that Roosevelt would be the nominee. What was in question was who his running mate would be. Vice President Henry Wallace was brilliant and idealistic, concerned about aiding the poor of the world, but he was also something of a religious mystic who got entangled in embarrassing situations. Some critics accused Wallace of having communist tendencies. If Roosevelt's health really was fragile, many Democratic leaders contended, they did not want to wake up one morning to find out that the erratic Wallace was president.

Privately, Roosevelt also believed Wallace must be

176

replaced. But in his typical way, he could not confront Wallace and say so straightforwardly. Instead he backed Wallace publicly while considering other candidates: James Byrnes, the Roosevelt aide who had been nicknamed "assistant president"; Sam Rayburn, Speaker of the House of Representatives; Missouri senator Harry S Truman; and Supreme Court justice William O. Douglas.

Behind the scenes Roosevelt indicated that he favored Truman, but he never said so publicly. He let both Byrnes and Wallace go to the convention in Chicago thinking that Roosevelt wanted them to win.

As the convention opened, Roosevelt was traveling to the West Coast—to visit military bases in California and later in Honolulu. As his train moved along, bitter fighting broke out among political leaders in Chicago over the question of his running mate. For a while it looked as if Byrnes would be the vice presidential choice; then Democratic officials decided that they must check first with Sidney Hillman, head of the CIO Political Action Committee, about their choices. Hillman favored Truman over Byrnes, and ultimately Truman became the nominee.

Eventually the story about Hillman became public, and there was much controversy over the fact that the Democrats had allowed a union official to decide who their vice presidential nominee would be. "Clear Everything With Sidney" became a Republican rallying cry during the campaign.

On July 19 the convention nominated Roosevelt. His acceptance speech was broadcast into the convention hall from Camp Pendleton in San Diego, where he sat in a car of his presidential train. Roosevelt closed his speech by quoting from Abraham Lincoln's second inaugural address: "With firmness in the right . . . let us strive on to finish the work we are in; to bind up the Nation's wounds . . . to do all which may achieve and cherish a just and lasting peace among ourselves, and with all Nations." [8]

Roosevelt had gone to the West Coast, partly to assure Californians that the war against the Japanese had not been forgotten in the excitement over D-Day. "These good people out here seem to feel a little neglected; for to them the Pacific operations seem at least as important as those in Normandy," he wrote in a letter at the time. "Their turn will come soon, I hope."[9]

After several days of inspections and sightseeing in California, Roosevelt went on to Honolulu to meet with such key military officers as Admiral Chester Nimitz and General Douglas MacArthur. Together they decided on the Philippines as the place where the Allied forces would make a major landing. From Hawaii Roosevelt sailed on the cruiser *Baltimore* to the Aleutian Islands off Alaska to visit with military men and do some fishing.

After sailing down the inland passage from Alaska to Puget Sound in Washington State, Roosevelt gave a speech aboard the destroyer *Cummings* to 10,000 shipyard workers and servicemen. Many who saw him that day were shocked at his appearance. His face was drawn and gray, and he spoke hesitantly. Although it was kept a secret for many years, he had suffered an angina attack of severe chest pains while he was speaking.

On other occasions, family members and associates noted that his hands shook while he ate and he had become absentminded and likely to repeat stories over and over again when he talked.

By the end of August, France had been liberated and American troops were marching through Paris. Victory in Europe seemed close at hand.

But Churchill and Roosevelt had begun to encounter ominous problems with the Soviet leader, Stalin. Stalin's actions did not bode well for what the Soviets would try to do in Europe after the war finally ended. One of the first signs of how brutal Stalin could be occurred after the Polish underground rose up in Warsaw against the Germans in August 1944. The Russians, who had pushed into Poland with their troops, refused to aid the underground

178

patriots and refused to let the Americans and British do so either. Stalin did not want Poles allied to the United States and Washington to take control of Poland. Eventually, the Germans killed more than a quarter million of these courageous Poles and devastated Warsaw.

At the Dumbarton Oaks conference, Stalin's associates also stubbornly insisted that each of the sixteen Soviet republics must have a vote if a United Nations were created. This would have given Stalin enormous power over the deliberations of the proposed United Nations.

In light of all this, Roosevelt's ambassador to Russia, Averell Harriman, feared that the Soviet Union would create serious difficulties after the war. But Roosevelt still believed that he could handle the Soviets and coax Stalin into doing what he wanted.

In fact, Roosevelt seemed more worried about the military threat that Germany might pose after the war. Could the Germans rise up again and resume their aggression in Europe, he wondered. In a letter to Queen Wilhelmina of Holland, Roosevelt said there were two views of Germany: "Those who would be altruistic in regard to the Germans, hoping by loving kindness to make them Christians again— and those who would adopt a much 'tougher' attitude. Most decidedly I belong to the latter school, for though I am not blood-thirsty, I want the Germans to know that this time at least they have definitely lost the war." [10]

The future fate of Germany was discussed by Roosevelt and Churchill in Quebec in mid-September. There they considered the Morgenthau Plan, proposed by Roosevelt's secretary of the treasury, Henry Morgenthau. The plan called for converting the heavily industrial Germany into an agricultural nation. At first Churchill was shocked because the idea seemed unworkable. Germany had never been able to grow enough food for itself and had always had to sell manufactured goods to buy imports. The plan would be like "chaining himself to a dead German," Churchill said. [11] But Churchill agreed to the plan after Morgenthau prom-

179

ised billions in new aid to England. Later protests from Secretary of State Hull and Secretary of War Stimson led Roosevelt to reconsider and the plan was dropped.

In the beginning the pressure of the war and his own health kept Roosevelt from campaigning seriously for a fourth term. But Roosevelt knew he faced a strong Republican opponent in 1944, New York governor Thomas E. Dewey, only forty-two years old. Dewey had made a name for himself by putting New York mobsters behind bars and had a reputation for energy, efficiency, and honesty.

At the end of September, Roosevelt began working on a major campaign speech to be given before the Teamsters Union at the Statler Hotel in Washington, D.C. There was a feeling of tension in the air as the hundreds of guests finished dinner and waited for Roosevelt to speak. Rumors about his ill health had spread for weeks. Did he still have the strength to be president? Was he going to be a pushover for Dewey?

At one table Roosevelt's daughter, Anna Boettiger, nervously asked Roosevelt's speech writer Sam Rosenman, "Do you think that Pa will put it over? If the delivery isn't just right, it'll be an awful flop." [12]

After a hesitant start, Roosevelt strongly attacked the Republicans. The liberals in the Republican party had never been able to drive out the Old Guard, he told the crowd, and the Old Guard could never pass itself off as the New Deal. "We have all seen many marvellous stunts in the circus, but no performing elephant could turn a hand-spring without falling flat on its back." [13]

The Republicans hadn't been happy just to attack his wife and sons and him, he said. "No, not content with that, they now include my little dog, Fala."

His opponents, he said, "had concocted a story that I had left him behind on an Aleutian Island and had sent a destroyer back to find him—at a cost to the taxpayers of two or three or eight or twenty million dollars—his Scotch soul was furious. He has not been the same dog since." [14]

The guests roared with laughter and applauded. Roosevelt had proved he was still a strong campaigner and an eloquent speaker. Somehow, in spite of his ill health, he would pull off this campaign, the Democrats believed.

Dewey, of course, viewed the speech as snide and personal and responded with sharp attacks on Roosevelt. Among other charges, he claimed that Roosevelt had the support of Communist leaders. Crowds were indeed turning out for Dewey, and campaign pledges were pouring into the Republican party.

At one point Dewey could have hit Roosevelt hard on the question of whether the president had advance warning about Pearl Harbor and could have prevented the destruction. But General George Marshall persuaded Dewey not to mention the situation during the campaign.

Toward the end of the campaign, events in the war turned Roosevelt's way. On October 20 he announced that General MacArthur had landed successfully in the Philippines. Then Roosevelt went on to a series of wildly successful campaign appearances. Between 1.5 million and 3 million people turned out to see him riding through the boroughs of New York City in an open car while rain drenched him, Eleanor, and Fala. At points on the parade route the Secret Service had to whisk Roosevelt into garages where they changed him into dry clothes. Enthusiastic crowds also greeted him in Philadelphia, Chicago, and Boston.

As short as it was, it was a trying and tiring campaign. Bad weather had pursued Roosevelt everywhere, and he had come to despise his opponent, Dewey, for his personal attacks. On Election Day Roosevelt returned to Hyde Park as usual. A houseful of guests were there to await the results. Shortly after eleven a torchlight parade of supporters marched to the Roosevelt mansion, and the president spoke to the crowd briefly. Finally, at 3:15 A.M. Dewey conceded. Although Roosevelt's margin of victory was narrower than ever before, it was not a close election.

Roosevelt received 53.5 percent of the popular vote, compared to 46 percent for Dewey.

Roosevelt returned triumphantly to Washington and then went on to recuperate from the campaign at Warm Springs. His next objective was to meet again with Churchill and Stalin to set the tone for the end of the war. Many questions remained to be answered about peacetime Germany and Eastern Europe.

17

"He did his job to the end"

On Inauguration Day, January 20, 1945, Roosevelt strapped himself painfully into his braces so that he could stand and deliver his speech, something he rarely did anymore and would not do again after the inaugural. Before the brief ceremony he talked to his son James about what should be done if he should die. "The first moment I saw Father I realized something was terribly wrong," James later said. "He looked awful and regardless of what the doctor said, I knew in my heart that his days were numbered." [1]

Meanwhile, in Europe, the Allied forces were pressing relentlessly against the shattered remnants of the German Army. Continual bombing by the Allies had reduced Berlin to rubble; although Hitler continued to talk about victory, his generals knew that the end was near. Regular bombing raids by American B-29s were now striking Tokyo as well. The Japanese Navy had also suffered severe setbacks in the South Pacific. In Los Alamos, New Mexico, the scientists working on the Manhattan Project to create the atomic bomb predicted that they were only months away from producing a bomb that could wield a new and unbelievable force.

With victory in sight that January, Roosevelt sailed off on the U.S.S. *Quincy* for his conference with Stalin and Churchill in Yalta in the Soviet Crimea. The trip was supposed to be a secret, but most Americans knew that some type of important high-level meeting was about to take place.

The long, grueling voyage took more than five weeks. To reach Yalta, Roosevelt traveled 14,000 miles by ship, plane, and car. Among those accompanying him was his daughter, Anna. She was very concerned about her father's health and what effect the trip might have on him.

On the way to Yalta the American officials met the British. Churchill and his doctor, Lord Moran, were shocked at how sick Roosevelt looked. Moran estimated that Roosevelt had only a few months to live.

But once in Yalta, Roosevelt seemed to bounce back a bit and rose to the challenge of these important meetings. The sessions were held in the luxurious Livadia Palace, a former residence of the czar of Russia on a site overlooking the Black Sea. Among the questions the three leaders considered was what would happen to Germany, whether the Soviet Union would enter the war against Japan, how the United Nations would operate, and what would happen to Poland.

Roosevelt and Churchill continued to have their differences. Roosevelt was intent on seeing an end to the British colonial empire; Churchill, on the other hand, favored maintaining a strong empire—partly to create a balance of power with the Soviet Union, which he feared would end up controlling all of Eastern Europe.

Certainly, Stalin was troubling on the question of Poland. Britain had entered the war to guarantee the freedom and independence of Poland, so the British wanted Polish officials in exile in London to have some say in the temporary government of a freed Poland. But Stalin had already set up a provisional government for Poland made up of Communist officials sympathetic to him and resisted having any London Poles involved. Churchill would not agree to Stalin's annexing some Polish territory unless Stalin agreed to free elections in Poland. Roosevelt also argued strongly for a new interim government for Poland combining moderate Poles from abroad with the Moscow-dominated Poles. But he was also well aware that the Soviet army was occupying all of Poland. After the meeting Roosevelt sent Stalin a note saying that "the United States will never lend its support in any way to any provisional government in Poland which would be inimical to your interests."[2]

Later, when Stalin made some concessions about the United Nations, Churchill also agreed to Stalin's territorial demands. In return, Stalin promised that he would allow some of the London Poles to have some say, but clearly, Stalin and the Communist government he had set up in Poland would remain in control.

Roosevelt admitted to advisers that the Polish compromise was a poor one, but he believed it was the best he could do. He probably did not expect that one day his critics would accuse him of selling out to Stalin or betraying Poland to the Soviets.

Regarding Germany, the three agreed to divide that country into four occupied zones—British, American, Soviet, and French. Stalin also demanded that the Germans pay $10 billion in reparations for war damages to the Soviet Union. Both Roosevelt and Churchill objected, but then Harry Hopkins, Roosevelt's aide, wrote a note to his boss: "Mr. President, the Russians have given in so much at this conference that I do not think we should let them down."[3]

Soon after, Roosevelt agreed to at least consider Russia's demand. Later, Stalin claimed that by this statement Roosevelt actually agreed to what the Soviets wanted.

The Americans were happy, though, over Stalin's

promise to enter the war against Japan. At the time, U.S. officials had no idea whether the atomic bomb would work or not and feared that the Allies might have to invade Japan to end the war. Such an invasion might cost as many as a half million dead and wounded. But if Russia could attack Japanese forces in Manchuria and north China, that might all change.

In return, Stalin asked for some territory in the Pacific—the Kurile Islands and the lower half of Sakhalin Island, as well as rights to other ports. Without consulting the Chinese, who actually had rights to these territories, Roosevelt agreed, but the agreement was kept secret until after his death some months later. When the word got out, there were many protests because Roosevelt, in yielding this territory to Stalin, seemed to violate all the principles he had been fighting for.

Also at the conference the "big three" agreed to the voting procedure for the United Nations Security Council. Their three governments plus France and China each were granted veto power over Security Council decisions. Roosevelt was pleased that Stalin agreed to join the United Nations and also that Stalin dropped his earlier demand that all sixteen Soviet republics have a vote in the General Assembly. Only three required votes, Stalin said, the Ukraine, White Russia, and Lithuania.

As a final step the leaders adopted the Declaration on Liberated Europe providing that they would help "form interim governmental authorities broadly representative of all democratic elements in the population." They also promised free elections as early as possible.[4]

But the promise meant nothing to Stalin; he ignored it as he dropped the Iron Curtain around the Eastern European countries of Poland, Romania, Bulgaria, and Hungary.

Roosevelt's role at Yalta has long been debated and criticized. If Roosevelt had been healthier, would the results have been different? Were he and his aides naive about

Stalin's ultimate intentions? Or did they give up on Poland and Eastern Europe purely because they knew they were lost anyway?

Probably the outcome of Yalta would have been the same regardless of how tough a stand Roosevelt had taken with Stalin. Thirty years later, Lord Galdwyn, an aide to Churchill at the conference, concluded: "If there hadn't been any Yalta Conference at all, the result would have been much the same. I think history would have fulfilled itself, Yalta or no Yalta." [5]

Roosevelt and Churchill were undoubtedly suspicious of Stalin, but they probably did not suspect how far he would go in violating their agreements.

On his return to the United States, Roosevelt went before Congress on March 1 to report the results of the conference. Appearing in the House of Representatives, he spoke to the joint Congress for the first time while sitting in an armchair. He apologized for the fact that he had not worn his braces to stand before the lawmakers. "I come from the Crimea Conference with a firm belief that we have made a good start on the road to a world of peace," he said. [6]

Although he still looked worn out and weak, the *New York Times* reported that he was tanned and well rested.

The next day Roosevelt went to Hyde Park for a brief rest and then took a train to Warm Springs, Georgia. Perhaps his favorite resort could bring him strength and relief. At times at Warm Springs, he seemed to brighten and look more lively. Then his spirits and health sank again. His secretary Grace Tully reported that on one occasion, "In two hours he seemed to have failed dangerously. His face was ashen, heightened by the darkening shadows under his eyes, and with his cheeks drawn gauntly." [7]

Despite his ill health, Eleanor did not go with him to Warm Springs. In fact, Lucy Mercer Rutherfurd was there for a visit, along with two of Roosevelt's women cousins. Lucy had brought with her a painter, Elizabeth Shoumatoff, who was painting a watercolor portrait of the president.

Roosevelt spent April 11 working on a radio speech he was to give on April 13. But in the afternoon he went for a drive with Lucy and his cousins. The next day, April 12, he did paperwork again while his visitors watched Elizabeth Shoumatoff painting his picture. At 1:15 P.M. he rubbed the back of his neck and said, "I have a terrific headache." He collapsed in his chair. After so many months of failing health, the end had come unexpectedly. He never regained consciousness although he was still breathing at first as the women rushed to his side. He is believed to have suffered a cerebral hemorrhage, or stroke.

Lucy quickly packed and left Warm Springs. She didn't want the rest of the world to know she was present when Roosevelt died. At 3:35 P.M. a doctor pronounced the president dead.

Eleanor had been at a party when she was given the news that something had happened to her husband. "I got into the car and sat with clenched hands all the way to the White House," she said. "In my heart of hearts I knew what had happened, but one does not actually formulate these terrible thoughts until they are spoken."[8]

Once she knew her husband was dead, she cabled her sons to say: "He did his job to the end as he would want you to do."[9]

Then she summoned Harry Truman, the vice president, to the White House to give him the news. Truman was shocked, but quickly took the oath of office. Although Roosevelt had known his health was declining, he had given Truman almost no preparation for the job of president. It was one of Roosevelt's greatest failures. The new president knew almost nothing about the agreements made at Yalta or about the atomic-bomb research going on in New Mexico.

Once Eleanor got to Warm Springs, she was told that Lucy Rutherfurd had been visiting when her husband died, but she gave no outward sign that she was hurt or angry over the news.

Partly because there had been so little discussion of Roosevelt's health and partly because of the deep affection that Americans held for their four-term president, the nation as a whole was deeply shocked by the news of the death. On April 13 a solemn funeral train, carrying Roosevelt's body, left Warm Springs for Washington and moved slowly through the South. Mourners swarmed to the stations and stood for hours to catch a glimpse of the train that held the man who had led the nation for so long and through so many deep waters of economic and wartime crisis.

Eleanor Roosevelt was on that train. "I lay in my berth all night with the window shade up," she later wrote, "looking out at the countryside he had loved and watching the faces of the people at stations, and even at the crossroads, who came to pay their last tribute all through the night."[10]

There was a funeral service first at the White House and then additional services at Hyde Park. Roosevelt's coffin was finally laid in a grave in the rose garden on the tree-covered estate next to the Hudson—a land he had cherished since his boyhood.

Perhaps the most notable and dynamic figure of the twentieth century had passed from the scene and left the entire world wondering what would happen next. America had put to rest the only president ever to be elected to four terms in office, a man who had built a new political coalition for the Democratic party that would hold on to power in the nation for decades to come.

Many Americans would remember him as the man who had put their nation on its feet again after a devastating depression had taken away the homes and jobs of millions. Others would remember his methods as dictatorial and would heap criticism on the tremendous growth in government spending and agencies that occurred during his administration. Certainly, the size and shape of the federal government and the kinds of tasks it undertook had been changed forever by Franklin Roosevelt.

Most Americans would remember his efforts to keep Europe free and to support England in the dark hours before World War II began. Others would criticize him for not doing enough to stop Hitler early on and to help Jewish refugees.

Almost everyone would acknowledge his spirited and forceful leadership during World War II and his determination to create a new world where all nations would be guaranteed independence and where a new United Nations would work to keep the peace. Others would criticize him for not holding the line against Joseph Stalin and the Soviet Union in Eastern Europe.

Regardless of their opinions, all would acknowledge that he had put his own personal stamp and signature on the nation and the world, and neither would ever be the same.

Source Notes

CHAPTER 1

1. Frank Burt Freidel, *Franklin Delano Roosevelt: The Apprenticeship* (Boston: Little, Brown, 1952), p. 20.
2. Ibid., p. 21.
3. Kenneth Sydney Davis, *FDR: The Beckoning of Destiny, 1882–1928* (New York: Putnam, 1972), p. 61.
4. Freidel, *FDR: The Apprenticeship*, p. 23.
5. Davis, p. 53.
6. Ibid., p. 63.
7. Freidel, *FDR: The Apprenticeship*, p. 33.
8. Ibid., p. 33.
9. *The Roosevelt Letters*, vol. 1, *Personal Correspondence of Franklin Delano Roosevelt, 1887–1904*, ed. Elliott Roosevelt (London: George G. Harrap, 1949), p. 97.
10. Ibid., p. 82.
11. Freidel, *FDR: The Apprenticeship*, p. 48.
12. *The Roosevelt Letters*, vol. 1, p. 206.
13. Freidel, *FDR: The Apprenticeship*, pp. 50–51.

CHAPTER 2

1. *The Roosevelt Letters*, vol. 1, *Personal Correspondence of Franklin Delano Roosevelt, 1887–1904,* ed. Elliott Roosevelt (London: George G. Harrap, 1949), p. 369.
2. Frank Burt Freidel, *Franklin Delano Roosevelt: The Apprenticeship* (Boston: Little, Brown, 1952), p. 57.
3. *The Roosevelt Letters*, vol. 1, p. 434.
4. Ibid., p. 439.
5. Joseph P. Lash, *Eleanor and Franklin: The Story of Their Relationship* (New York: W. W. Norton, 1971), p. 61.
6. Ibid., p. 108.
7. Eleanor Roosevelt, *This Is My Story* (New York: Harper, 1937), p. 111.

CHAPTER 3

1. Joseph P. Lash, *Eleanor and Franklin: The Story of Their Relationship* (New York: W. W. Norton, 1971), p. 109.
2. *The Roosevelt Letters,* vol. 1, *Personal Correspondence of Franklin Delano Roosevelt, 1887–1904,* ed. Elliott Roosevelt (London: George G. Harrap, 1949), p. 442.
3. Ibid., p. 443.
4. *The Roosevelt Letters,* vol. 2, *Personal Correspondence of Franklin Delano Roosevelt, 1905–1928,* ed. Elliott Roosevelt (London: George G. Harrap, 1950), p. 73.
5. Frank Burt Freidel, *Franklin Delano Roosevelt: The Apprenticeship* (Boston: Little, Brown, 1952), p. 86.
6. Eleanor Roosevelt, *This Is My Story* (New York: Harper, 1938), p. 162.
7. *The Roosevelt Letters*, vol. 2, p. 130.
8. Ibid., p. 137.
9. Ibid., p. 140.
10. Ibid., p. 143.
11. Frances Perkins, *The Roosevelt I Knew* (New York: Viking Press, 1946), p. 11.
12. Ibid., p. 12.
13. Ibid., p. 14.

CHAPTER 4

1. *The Roosevelt Letters,* vol. 2, *Personal Correspondence of Franklin Delano Roosevelt, 1905–1928,* ed. Elliott Roosevelt (London: George G. Harrap, 1950), p. 170.
2. Kenneth Sydney Davis, *FDR: The Beckoning of Destiny, 1882–1928* (New York: Putnam, 1972), p. 321.
3. Ibid., p. 336.
4. Ibid., p. 339.
5. *The Roosevelt Letters,* vol. 2, p. 195.
6. Ibid., p. 204.
7. Davis, *FDR: The Beckoning of Destiny, 1882–1928,* p. 389.
8. *The Roosevelt Letters,* vol. 2, p. 212.
9. Frank Burt Freidel, *Franklin Delano Roosevelt: The Apprenticeship* (Boston: Little, Brown, 1952), p. 291.
10. Ibid., p. 300.
11. Ibid., p. 321.
12. *The Roosevelt Letters,* vol. 2, p. 348.

CHAPTER 5

1. Geoffrey C. Ward, *A First Class Temperament: The Emergence of Franklin Roosevelt* (New York: Harper & Row, 1989), p. 477.
2. Ibid., p. 511.
3. Ibid., p. 521.
4. *The Roosevelt Letters,* vol. 2, *Personal Correspondence of Franklin Delano Roosevelt, 1905–1928,* ed. Elliott Roosevelt (London: George G. Harrap, 1950), p. 398.
5. Joseph P. Lash, *Eleanor and Franklin: The Story of Their Relationship* (New York: W. W. Norton, 1971), p. 256.
6. Ward, *A First Class Temperament,* p. 557.
7. Kenneth Sydney Davis, *FDR: The Beckoning of Destiny, 1882–1928* (New York: Putnam, 1972), p. 643.

CHAPTER 6

1. Kenneth Sydney Davis, *FDR: The Beckoning of Destiny, 1882–1928* (New York: Putnam, 1972), p. 648.
2. *The Roosevelt Letters,* vol. 2, *Personal Correspondence of Franklin Delano Roosevelt, 1905–1928,* ed. Elliott Roosevelt (London: George G. Harrap, 1950), p. 411.

3. Ibid., p. 414.
4. Jean Gould, *A Good Fight: The Story of FDR's Conquest of Polio* (New York: Dodd, Mead, 1960), p. 69.
5. Frank Burt Freidel, *Franklin Delano Roosevelt: The Ordeal* (Boston: Little, Brown, 1954), p. 100.
6. *The Roosevelt Letters*, vol. 2, p. 418.
7. James Roosevelt with Bill Libby, *My Parents: A Differing View* (Chicago: Playboy Press, 1976), p. 74.
8. Frances Perkins, *The Roosevelt I Knew* (New York: Viking Press, 1946), p. 29.
9. James Roosevelt, p. 95.
10. Ibid., p. 82.
11. Eleanor Roosevelt, *This Is My Story* (New York: Harper, 1937), p. 339.
12. James Roosevelt, p. 75.
13. Geoffrey C. Ward, *A First Class Temperament: The Emergence of Franklin Roosevelt* (New York: Harper & Row, 1989), pp. 616–617.

CHAPTER 7

1. James Roosevelt with Bill Libby, *My Parents: A Differing View* (Chicago: Playboy Press, 1976), p. 85.
2. Ibid., p. 105.
3. Eleanor Roosevelt, *This I Remember* (New York: Harper, 1949), p. 27.
4. *The Roosevelt Letters*, vol. 2, *Personal Correspondence of Franklin Delano Roosevelt, 1905–1928*, ed. Elliott Roosevelt (London: George G. Harrap, 1950), p. 442.
5. James Roosevelt, p. 93.
6. *The Roosevelt Letters*, vol. 2, p. 443.

CHAPTER 8

1. *The Roosevelt Letters*, vol. 2, *Personal Correspondence of Franklin Delano Roosevelt, 1905–1928*, ed. Elliott Roosevelt (London: George G. Harrap, 1950), p. 503.
2. Ibid.
3. Kenneth Sydney Davis, *FDR: The Beckoning of Destiny, 1882–1928* (New York: Putnam, 1972), pp. 822–823.
4. Geoffrey C. Ward, *A First Class Temperament: The Emer-*

gence of Franklin Roosevelt (New York: Harper & Row, 1989), p. 790.
5. Joseph P. Lash, *Eleanor and Franklin: The Story of Their Relationship* (New York: W. W. Norton, 1971), p. 317.
6. Davis, *FDR: The Beckoning of Destiny*, p. 850.
7. Ernest K. Lindley, *Franklin Delano Roosevelt: A Career in Progressive Democracy* (New York: Bobbs-Merrill, 1931), p. 20.
8. Ibid.
9. *The Roosevelt Letters*, vol. 2, p. 509.
10. Frank Burt Freidel, *Franklin Delano Roosevelt: The Ordeal* (Boston: Little, Brown, 1954), p. 255.
11. Ward, *A First Class Temperament*, p. 794.
12. Freidel, *FDR: The Ordeal*, p. 257.
13. *The Roosevelt Letters*, vol. 2, p. 510.
14. Hugh Gregory Gallagher, *FDR's Splendid Deception* (New York: Dodd, Mead, 1985), p. 73.
15. Frances Perkins, *The Roosevelt I Knew* (New York: Viking Press, 1946), p. 48.

CHAPTER 9

1. Kenneth Sydney Davis, *FDR: The New York Years, 1928–1933* (New York: Random House, 1985), pp. 60–61.
2. Ibid., p. 154.
3. Frank Burt Freidel, *Franklin Delano Roosevelt: The Triumph* (Boston: Little, Brown, 1956), p. 164.
4. Frances Perkins, *The Roosevelt I Knew* (New York: Viking Press, 1946).
5. Ibid., p. 108.

CHAPTER 10

1. *The Roosevelt Letters*, vol. 3, *Personal Correspondence of Franklin Delano Roosevelt, 1928–1945*, ed. Elliott Roosevelt (London: George G. Harrap, 1952), p. 41.
2. Ibid., p. 85.
3. Ibid., p. 75.
4. Frank Burt Freidel, *Franklin Delano Roosevelt: The Triumph* (Boston: Little, Brown, 1956), p. 210.
5. Ibid., p. 249.

6. Ibid., p. 251.
7. Arthur M. Schlesinger, Jr., *The Age of Roosevelt: The Crisis of the Old Order, 1919–1933* (Boston: Houghton Mifflin, 1957), p. 292.
8. Ibid., p. 313.
9. Freidel, *FDR: The Triumph*, p. 315.
10. Schlesinger, p. 420.
11. Ibid., p. 416.
12. Freidel, *FDR: The Triumph*, p. 354.
13. Ibid., p. 358.
14. Schlesinger, *Age of R.: The Crisis of the Old Order*, p. 431.
15. Ibid., p. 434.
16. Ibid., p. 439.

CHAPTER 11

1. Frances Perkins, *The Roosevelt I Knew* (New York: Viking Press, 1946), p. 140.
2. Frank Burt Freidel, *Franklin Delano Roosevelt: Launching the New Deal* (Boston: Little, Brown, 1973), pp. 202–205.
3. Perkins, p. 153.
4. Arthur M. Schlesinger, Jr., *The Age of Roosevelt: The Coming of the New Deal* (Boston: Houghton Mifflin, 1959), p. 13.
5. Ibid., p. 63.
6. Ibid., p. 201.
7. Ibid., p. 102.
8. Ibid., pp. 264–265.
9. Ibid., p. 274.

CHAPTER 12

1. Arthur M. Schlesinger, Jr., *The Age of Roosevelt: The Coming of the New Deal* (Boston: Houghton Mifflin, 1959), p. 505.
2. Eleanor Roosevelt, *This I Remember* (New York: Harper, 1949), p. 68.
3. Schlesinger, *Age of R.: The Coming of the New Deal*, p. 311.
4. Frances Perkins, *The Roosevelt I Knew* (New York: Viking Press, 1946), p. 301.

5. Frank Burt Freidel, *Franklin Delano Roosevelt: A Rendezvous With Destiny* (Boston: Little, Brown, 1990), p. 161.
6. Ibid., p. 163.
7. Eleanor Roosevelt, *This I Remember*, p. 82.
8. Ibid., p. 69.
9. Ibid., p. 162.
10. Freidel, *FDR: A Rendezvous With Destiny*, p. 246.
11. Eleanor Roosevelt, *This I Remember*, p. 165.
12. Schlesinger, *Age of R.: The Coming of the New Deal*, p. 537.
13. Ibid.

CHAPTER 13

1. Eleanor Roosevelt, *This I Remember* (New York: Harper, 1949), p. 145.
2. Frank Burt Freidel, *Franklin Delano Roosevelt: A Rendezvous With Destiny* (Boston: Little, Brown 1990), p. 202.
3. Ibid., p. 207.
4. Eleanor Roosevelt, *This I Remember*, p. 147.
5. *The Roosevelt Letters*, vol. 3, *Personal Correspondence of Franklin Delano Roosevelt, 1928–1945*, ed. Elliott Roosevelt (London: George G. Harrap, 1952), p. 200.
6. William E. Leuchtenburg, *Franklin D. Roosevelt and the New Deal* (New York: Harper & Row, 1963), p. 233.
7. Freidel, *FDR: A Rendezvous With Destiny*, p. 229.
8. Leuchtenburg, p. 238.
9. Freidel, *FDR: A Rendezvous With Destiny*, p. 282.

CHAPTER 14

1. Frank Burt Freidel, *Franklin Delano Roosevelt: A Rendezvous With Destiny* (Boston: Little, Brown, 1990), p. 264.
2. William E. Leuchtenburg, *Franklin D. Roosevelt and the New Deal* (New York: Harper & Row, 1963), p. 230.
3. Robert Leckie, *Delivered From Evil: The Saga of World War II* (New York: Harper & Row, 1987), p. 71.
4. *The Roosevelt Letters*, vol. 3, *Personal Correspondence of Franklin Delano Roosevelt, 1928–1945*, ed. Elliott Roosevelt (London: George G. Harrap, 1952), p. 241.
5. Freidel, *FDR: A Rendezvous With Destiny*, p. 322.

6. Ibid., p. 345.
7. Ibid., p. 355.
8. James MacGregor Burns, *Roosevelt: The Soldier of Freedom, 1940–1945* (New York: Harcourt Brace Jovanovich, 1970), p. 26.
9. Ibid., p. 28.
10. Eleanor Roosevelt, *This I Remember* (New York: Harper, 1949), p. 227.

CHAPTER 15

1. Frank Burt Freidel, *Franklin Delano Roosevelt: A Rendezvous With Destiny* (Boston: Little, Brown, 1990), p. 402.
2. Eleanor Roosevelt, *This I Remember* (New York: Harper, 1949), p. 233.
3. James MacGregor Burns, *Roosevelt: The Soldier of Freedom, 1940–1945* (New York: Harcourt Brace Jovanovich, 1970), pp. 165–167.
4. Ibid., p. 212.
5. Freidel, *FDR: A Rendezvous With Destiny*, p. 457.
6. Ibid., p. 462.
7. Burns, p. 323.
8. Ibid.
9. Robert Leckie, *Delivered From Evil: The Saga of World War II* (New York: Harper & Row, 1987), p. 512.

CHAPTER 16

1. Frank Burt Freidel, *Franklin Delano Roosevelt: A Rendezvous With Destiny* (Boston: Little, Brown, 1990), p. 482.
2. James MacGregor Burns, *Roosevelt: The Soldier of Freedom, 1940–1945* (New York: Harcourt Brace Jovanovich, 1970), p. 413.
3. Freidel, *FDR: A Rendezvous With Destiny*, p. 490.
4. Joseph P. Lash, *Eleanor and Franklin: The Story of Their Relationship* (New York: W. W. Norton, 1971), p. 694.
5. Ibid., p. 695.
6. Burns, p. 425.
7. Ibid., p. 476.
8. Ibid., p. 507.
9. *The Roosevelt Letters*, vol. 3, *Personal Correspondence of*

Franklin Delano Roosevelt, 1928–1945, ed. Elliott Roosevelt (London: George G. Harrap, 1952), p. 504.

10. Ibid., p. 509.
11. Robert Leckie, *Delivered From Evil: The Saga of World War II* (New York: Harper & Row, 1987), p. 774.
12. Burns, p. 521.
13. Ibid., p. 522.
14. Ibid., pp. 523–524.

CHAPTER 17

1. Hugh Gregory Gallagher, *FDR's Splendid Deception* (New York: Dodd, Mead, 1985), p. 199.
2. Robert Leckie, *Delivered From Evil: The Saga of World War II* (New York: Harper & Row, 1987), p. 846.
3. Ibid., p. 848.
4. Frank Burt Freidel, *Franklin Delano Roosevelt: A Rendezvous With Destiny* (Boston: Little, Brown, 1990), p. 589.
5. Gallagher, p. 205.
6. Freidel, *FDR: A Rendezvous With Destiny*, p. 598.
7. Gallagher, p. 208.
8. Joseph P. Lash, *Eleanor and Franklin: The Story of Their Relationship* (New York: W. W. Norton, 1971), p. 721.
9. Ibid.
10. Ibid., p. 732.

For Further Reading

Burns, James MacGregor. *Roosevelt: The Soldier of Freedom, 1940–1945*. New York: Harcourt Brace Jovanovich, 1970.

Davis, Kenneth Sydney. *FDR: The Beckoning of Destiny, 1882–1928*. New York: Putnam, 1972.

———. *FDR: The New York Years 1928–1933*. New York: Random House, 1985.

———. *FDR: The New Deal Years 1933–1937*. New York: Random House, 1986.

Freidel, Frank Burt. *Franklin Delano Roosevelt: The Apprenticeship*. Boston: Little, Brown, 1952.

———. *Franklin Delano Roosevelt: Launching the New Deal*. Boston: Little, Brown, 1973.

———. *Franklin Delano Roosevelt: The Ordeal*. Boston: Little, Brown, 1954.

———. *Franklin Delano Roosevelt: A Rendezvous With Destiny*. Boston: Little, Brown, 1990.

———. *Franklin Delano Roosevelt: The Triumph*. Boston: Little, Brown, 1956.

Gallagher, Hugh Gregory. *FDR's Splendid Deception*. New York: Dodd, Mead, 1985.

Gould, Jean. *A Good Fight: The Story of FDR's Conquest of Polio*. New York: Dodd, Mead, 1960.

Lash, Joseph P. *Eleanor and Franklin: The Story of Their Relationship*. New York: W. W. Norton, 1971.

Leckie, Robert. *Delivered From Evil: The Saga of World War II*. New York: Harper & Row, 1987.

Leuchtenburg, William E. *Franklin D. Roosevelt and the New Deal*. New York: Harper & Row, 1963.

Morgan, Ted. *FDR: A Biography*. New York: Simon and Schuster, 1985.

Perkins, Frances. *The Roosevelt I Knew*. New York: Viking Press, 1946.

Roosevelt, Eleanor. *This I Remember*. New York: Harper, 1949.

———. *This Is My Story*. New York: Harper, 1937.

Roosevelt, James, with Bill Libby. *My Parents: A Differing View*. Chicago: Playboy Press, 1976.

The Roosevelt Letters, Personal Correspondence of Franklin Delano Roosevelt, 1887–1904 (vol. 1), *1905–1928* (vol. 2), *1928–1945* (vol. 3). Ed. Elliott Roosevelt. London: George C. Harrap, 1949, 1950, 1952.

Schlesinger, Arthur M., Jr. *The Age of Roosevelt: The Coming of the New Deal*. Boston: Houghton Mifflin, 1959.

———. *The Age of Roosevelt: The Crisis of the Old Order, 1919–1933*. Boston: Houghton Mifflin, 1957.

———. *The Age of Roosevelt: The Politics of Upheaval*. Boston: Houghton Mifflin, 1960.

Ward, Geoffrey C. *Before the Trumpet: The Young Franklin Roosevelt, 1882–1905*. New York: Harper & Row, 1985.

———. *A First Class Temperament: The Emergence of Franklin Roosevelt*. New York: Harper & Row, 1989.

Index

Clark, Champ, 38
Cleveland, Grover, 15
Columbia Law School, 29–31
Congress, U.S., 11, 14, 18, 34, 43, 46, 51, 52, 57–58, 91, 113, 114, 115, 117, 120, 123–25, 129, 130, 132, 135, 137–43, 145–54, 158–59, 162, 171, 173, 174, 187
Connell, Richard E., 34
Constitution, U.S., 80, 115, 136, 137–38, 140, 146
Coolidge, Calvin, 56, 74
Coughlin, Rev. Charles, 113, 122, 136
Cox, James M., 53–54, 56
Crash of 1929, 89–90, 93
Czechoslovakia, 146–47, 148

Daniels, Josephus, 40–44, 46–48, 52, 53
Darlan, Jean-François, 165
Davis, John W., 77, 136
Davis, Livingston, 41, 47, 48
De Gaulle, Charles, 165, 167, 176
Delano, Fred, 61, 63, 64
Depression, Great, 89–98, 100, 104, 105, 109–30, 134, 137–42

Dewey, Thomas E., 180, 181–82
Dickerman, Marion, 69, 89
Douglas, William O., 140, 177

Eisenhower, Dwight D., 163, 165, 176
Election of 1920, 53–56
Election of 1924, 74–77, 79
Election of 1928, 78, 79–87
Election of 1932, 82, 93, 94, 97–108
Election of 1936, 82, 134–37
Election of 1940, 141, 149–53
Election of 1944, 172, 173, 175–77, 180–82
Emergency Banking Act, 113–14, 115

Farley, James, 85, 98, 99, 101, 102, 107, 112, 137, 149, 150
Farm Credit Administration (FCA), 116, 126
Federal Deposit Insurance Corporation (FDIC), 126
Federal Emergency Relief Administration (FERA), 120, 126
Federal Housing Administration (FHA), 126

Federal Reserve System, 130

Federal Theatre Project, 123

Federal Writers' Project, 123–24

Fidelity and Deposit Company of Maryland, 56–57, 67, 71

Fireside chats, 114–15, 142, 149, 154

Flynn, Ed, 83, 101, 102, 107

Fourteen Points, 50, 51

France, 147–50, 165–66, 167, 175–76, 178, 185, 186

Franco, Francisco, 144, 154

Frankfurter, Felix, 105, 140

Gannett, Frank, 141

Gardner, Augustus P., 44

Garner, John Nance, 100, 101, 102–3, 105, 124, 136, 138, 149, 150

Gerard, James, 43

Germany, 143–56, 159, 160, 163–68, 171, 172, 176, 178–80, 182–85

Giraud, Henri, 166, 167

Great Britain, 10, 145, 147–50, 153–55, 160–63, 168, 171, 175, 179, 180, 184, 185, 190

Groton, 16–21, 23, 24, 26, 29, 30, 111

Harding, Warren, 52, 56, 57, 74

Harvard *Crimson,* 21–22

Harvard University, 19, 20–25, 27, 29, 41

Hillman, Sidney, 177

Hitler, Adolf, 141, 144, 145–50, 154, 155, 159, 165, 168, 183, 190

Home Owners' Loan Act, 118

Hoover, Herbert, 53, 82, 86, 90–91, 93, 94, 96, 101, 103, 106, 107, 110, 112, 114, 115, 131

Hopkins, Harry L., 96, 120–21, 123, 135, 142, 149, 154, 155, 157, 158, 185

Howe, Louis McHenry, 38–39, 41, 54–55, 57, 61, 64, 65, 67, 68, 70, 74, 75, 78, 81–85, 87, 97, 101, 102, 107–8, 112, 130, 131, 135

Howell, Clark, 98–99

Hughes, Charles Evans, 45–46, 128, 139

Hull, Cordell, 112, 133, 144, 149, 150, 180

Ickes, Harold, 112, 119, 120, 123

India, 161–62
Italy, 144, 145, 148, 154, 155, 159, 166, 167, 168

Japan, 143, 145, 146, 157–63, 167–69, 171, 178, 183, 184, 186
Jews, 144, 147, 190
Johnson, Hugh, 118–19
Joseph, Lewis, 71–72

Keen, W. W., 61
Kennedy, Joseph P., 123
Knox, Frank, 151

Landon, Alf, 135–36
League of Nations, 46, 50, 51, 52, 54–56, 100, 145
LeHand, Marguerite "Missy," 67, 68, 70–71, 84, 130, 156
Lehman, Herbert, 83–85, 88
Lend-Lease plan, 153–54
Lewis, John L., 152
Lincoln, Abraham, 34, 177
Lindbergh, Charles, 148–49
Lodge, Henry Cabot, 44, 51
Long, Huey, 113, 122, 129, 136
Lovett, Robert Williamson, 62, 71
Ludlow amendment, 146
Lusitania, 45

MacArthur, Douglas, 161, 178, 181
McIntire, Ross, 174–75
Marshall, George, 163, 166, 181
Mercer, Lucy Page, 48–49, 69, 71, 132, 174, 187–89
Moley, Raymond, 85, 104
Morgenthau, Henry, Jr., 85, 88, 179–80
Moses, Robert, 88, 95
Munich Pact, 146–47
Murphy, Charles F., 35, 54
Mussolini, Benito, 144, 148, 168

National Industrial Recovery Act, 118, 128
National Labor Relations Act, 129, 139
National Labor Relations Board (NLRB), 126–27, 129
National Recovery Administration (NRA), 118–20, 122, 127–29
National War Labor Board (NWLB), 127, 164
National Youth Administration (NYA), 124, 127
Neutrality Act, 147, 148
New Deal, 104, 110, 112–30, 134–43, 173–74, 180

Roosevelt, Theodore
  (cousin), 18, 19, 21–23,
  25, 27, 30, 31, 33, 34,
  38, 40–42, 46, 47, 51, 56
Rosenman, Samuel, 85,
  88, 103, 104, 180
Rutherfurd, Lucy Mercer.
  See Mercer, Lucy

Schlesinger, Arthur, Jr.,
  97–98, 133
Securities and Exchange
  Commission (SEC), 123,
  127, 129
Selective Service Act,
  152–53
Sheehan, William "Blue-
  Eyed Billy," 35–36
Shoumatoff, Elizabeth,
  187–88
Shouse, Jouett, 99, 122
Smith, Al, 73–77, 79–86,
  88–89, 98–103, 122, 136
Social Security system,
  125, 127, 140
Soil Conservation and Do-
  mestic Allotment Act,
  134
Soviet Union, 148, 155,
  159, 163–65, 168, 171,
  172, 175, 178–79, 184–
  87, 190
Spanish-American War,
  17–18, 41–42
Stabilization Act, 164
Stalin, Joseph, 148, 155,

159, 163–64, 166, 169–
  72, 178–79, 182, 184–
  87, 190
Stimson, Henry L., 93,
  151, 163, 180
Supreme Court, U.S.,
  128–29, 134, 136–40

Taft, Robert, 151
Taft, William Howard, 34
Tammany Hall, 35–37, 43,
  54, 92, 93, 100, 101–2
Tehran conference, 169,
  170–72, 173
Temporary Emergency Re-
  lief Administration, 96
Tennessee Valley Authority
  (TVA), 117–18, 127,
  151
Townsend, Francis, 113,
  125, 136
Treaty of Versailles, 50–
  52, 144, 145, 166
Truman, Harry S, 177, 188
Truth-in-Securities Act, 118
Tuttle, Charles H., 93–94
Tydings, Millard, 142, 152

United Nations, 171, 175,
  179, 184–86, 190

Van Devanter, Willis, 128,
  139, 140

Wagner, Robert, 129
Walker, Jimmy, 92, 93